NEW DEAL DAYS:
1933-1934

NEW DEAL DAYS: 1933-1934

Eli Ginzberg

TRANSACTION PUBLISHERS
New Brunswick (U.S.A.) and London (U.K.)

Copyright © 1997 by Transaction Publishers, New Brunswick, New Jersey 08903.

All rights reserved under International and Pan-American Copyright Conventions. No part of this book may be reproduced or transmitted in any form or by any means, electronic or mechanical, including photocopy, recording, or any information storage and retrieval system, without prior permission in writing from the publisher. All inquiries should be addressed to Transaction Publishers, Rutgers—The State University, New Brunswick, New Jersey 08903.

This book is printed on acid-free paper that meets the American National Standard for Permanence of Paper for Printed Library Materials.

Library of Congress Catalog Number: 97-2259
ISBN: 1-56000-331-6
Printed in the United States of America

Library of Congress Cataloging-in-Publication Data

Ginzberg, Eli, 1911–
  New Deal days, 1933–1934 / Eli Ginzberg.
    p. cm.
  ISBN 1-56000-331-6 (alk. paper)
  1. United States—Economic conditions—1918–1945. 2. United States—Social conditions—1933–1945. 3. New Deal, 1933–1939. I. Title.
HC106.3.G513 1997
338.973'009'043—dc21   97-2259
                                                                    CIP

To my Columbia University teachers and friends

Adolph A. Berle
Thomas C. Blaisdell
John Maurice Clark
Raymond Moley
Rexford Guy Tugwell
Leo Wolman

who made it possible for me to see the New Deal from the inside in 1933–34.

Contents

	Setting the Stage	1
1.	The New Deal	5
2.	Big Business	23
3.	The University	37
4.	Southwest	53
5.	Hollywood	69
6.	People and Places	83

Setting the Stage

The sketches that comprise this volume were written in 1933–34, the year that I travelled through the United States visiting the headquarters of forty large corporations including General Electric, Eastman Kodak, U.S. Steel, Standard Oil of New Jersey (Exxon), General Motors, Sears Roebuck, Goodyear Tire and Rubber, International Harvester and many others. I visited forty states during a ten-month trip during which I covered 40,000 miles.

Having successfully defended my doctoral dissertation, *The House of Adam Smith* (Columbia University Press, 1934) in the spring of 1933; having been awarded a William Bayard Cutting Traveling Fellowship that spring, I persuaded the Columbia University authorities to allow me to spend my Cutting year visiting large U.S. corporations rather than "absorbing culture" in London, Paris, and Rome in accordance with established practice for Cutting fellows. The fact that I had studied at Heidelberg and Grenoble some years earlier helped to persuade the Columbia authorities.

In seeking a change in venue I stressed in my request that having spent the last years attending lectures and reading books about economics, I felt an urgency to learn first hand about how the U.S. economy had weathered the most devastating depression in the nation's history and how it was responding to President Roosevelt's New Deal initiatives.

I had considered seeking a publisher for this volume in 1934, but one of my favorite professors had advised me against doing so pointing out that it would not be helpful for a young scholar starting on an academic career to be identified as the author of a nonscholarly output. On several occasions in the following decades I considered whether the manuscript might be published but I was unable to locate a copy either in my files at home or at Columbia. Recently it showed up on my desk at home probably as a consequence of housecleaning after my wife Ruth's death in the late summer of 1995.

My field investigations in 1933–34 resulted in a scholarly tome—*The Illusion of Economic Stability* that Harper and Brothers published in 1939. But I believe that the sketches that comprise this volume which reflect the impressions, reflections, and reactions of a provincial New Yorker in his first encounters with the South, Midwest, Southwest, and West in the months that President Roosevelt and his advisors were struggling to turn the nation around after its severe buffeting from the Great Depression may be of interest to various readers, the overwhelming majority of whom have no first hand knowledge of the Great Depression (1929–1933), the greatest domestic crisis in the nation's history, the Civil War alone excepted, and the beginnings of the New Deal that FDR initiated in 1933–34.

The William Cutting Traveling Fellowship that I received in the spring of 1933 carried a stipend of $1800 payable in two installments. As a close reader will observe I was preoccupied during most of my fellowship year with the possible, even likely, failure of the New Deal, which I feared would unleash a major inflation such as I had encountered on a trip to Germany as an eleven-year-old in 1922 when the mark had declined from 4 to 250 to the dollar, before it took off in the following year to a point when the value of paper on which the currency was printed exceeded its designated monetary value. The fact that I had studied "Money and Banking" with H. Parker Willis at Columbia—who had served as senior staff advisor to Senator Carter Glass at the time when the senator was steering the Federal Reserve Act through the Senate (1913) also made me a "hard money" man fearful of any and all tampering with the value of the dollar.

To underscore my disquietude about how the New Deal initiatives might undermine the value of the dollar consider the following. On receipt of the first installment of my fellowship money I wrote to Harry George Friedman (latterly the president of General American Investors) and a life-long friend of my parents to please buy me some conservative stocks so that I would be able to afford the skyrocketing prices for gasoline that I feared would prevail when I got ready to drive back East after the New Year from California. I recall his reply: "You are sufficiently young not to realize that logic governs neither the actions of men nor the gyrations of the stock market. However in accordance with your request I have bought today 25 shares of Endicott-Johnson stock for your account."

I recall my principal mentor at Columbia University Wesley Clair Mitchell telling me that Willis had never altered his views on inflation since the time when they were graduate students at the University of Chicago shortly after the turn of the century. I too never shook off my early fears of inflation, based on my visit to Germany in 1922, a fear that led me to misdiagnose many developments before and after the onset of the New Deal.

A few points about dollars and prices in the early days of the New Deal. My mother, who did not drive, located a 1926 Buick sedan with a price tag of $200 which I bought. After driving it for 40,000 miles I was able to sell it for scrap on my return to New York City in May 1934 for $40. If my memory does not play me false I was able to buy six gallons of gas for one dollar most of the year that I was in the field except that I recall that in Los Angeles the price dropped to eight gallons for the dollar.

Since I was interviewing senior corporate executives some of whom might have occasion to telephone me I had to put up at a respectable hotel. With very few exceptions I was able to obtain accommodations for $1.50 per night, with no extra charge for parking my car usually at the rear of the hotel. In Detroit, which was seriously overbuilt with hotel accommodations, I paid for six nights for a seven-night stay.

One could get a multicourse breakfast usually at one of the chain drugstores for twenty-nine cents—fruit, eggs, toast, and coffee. Except when I was on the road I was always a guest at lunch, and frequently at dinner. After eleven months in the field I returned to New York City with several hundred dollars of my fellowship grant still unspent; in part because in Los Angeles I was a guest during a three-week stay with old friends from New York City who had relocated.

There was a great deal askew with the U.S. economy in the early days of the New Deal but hotel rooms, meals, gasoline were surely within the reach of the lucky ones like myself who had been awarded a liberal fellowship by a major university; and who spent the year interacting mostly with executives at their corporate headquarters and at their homes.

1

The New Deal

WITCHES' BREW

"Roosevelt et al.—why it is a Kulak administration trying to save the country for the Kulaks—and it's no small job."

The money changers were driven from the temple but Washington real estate agents maintain that they have never before been forced to deal with as unpleasant a group as swarmed into Washington with the new administration. True, there are not many Andrew Mellons and Ogden Mills in the new entourage but people with means are not rare; and these individuals are determined to rent $15,000 residences for $5,000.

Lest it be forgotten. It was Herbert Hoover who started the Reconstruction Finance Corporation (RFC)—"An organization dedicated to the noble efforts of letting smart money get out while the government held the bag." Mr. Hoover was probably stampeded into action by the moans and groans of the Wall Street bankers. They explained that if the government did not aid the railroads many securities would go into default and the widows and orphans throughout the land would soon be destitute. No humanitarian could withstand such an appeal.

The wise remember while the ignorant forget. "Roosevelt and Hoover—there is but one major difference—that of consistency." Farm relief was long a mainstay of Republican policies; open-market operations were not unknown to Mr. Mellon; the Republican attorney generals were not unduly concerned about the antitrust statutes; Mr. Hoover was long an advocate of public work programs in depressions. But Mr. Hoover was fearful, uncertain and therefore inconsistent. The Farm Board lost several hundred millions of dollars and then called a halt to its purchases; the Federal Reserve System bought government bonds in large amounts and then turned around and began to sell them; an occasional threat of prosecution against a monopoly and then an amiable conference.

But Mr. Roosevelt is determined, assured, and keeps pushing ahead. Agricultural commodities are destroyed; inflation of credit is pursued with a vengeance; the antitrust statutes are officially suspended; billions are spent in priming the pump. *Vanitas, vanitorum...*

* * *

Prior to the signing of the Steel Code, there were submitted to the National Recovery Administration (NRA) a large number of petitions from the steel workers begging the administration to force the companies to cancel all outstanding debts against their employees. Those who signed the petition, and there were several thousand, had worked an average of twelve years for the steel company to which they were in debt!

Critics of the administration have been prone to attack the increasing size and complexity of the federal bureaucracy. But they have been both shortsighted and unfair.

If the New Deal should falter, then, the NRA could prove that it was hampered by the ridiculously high wages that the Civil Works Administration (CWA) insisted on paying. The Agricultural Adjustment Act (AAA) could sustain in any court of law that its program was scuttled by the price rises that the NRA engendered. The Federal Emergency Relief Act (FERA) would have little difficulty in pointing out that a lack of funds hampered its activities. And the Treasury could convince even the uninformed that a balanced budget was impossible as long as the extraordinary expenditures of the government were not curtailed.

Hence, the bureaucracy will be vindicated, if not in life, then in death.

* * *

The administrator of the NRA, General Hugh S. Johnson, was an army man and that probably explained his distaste for the intellectuals who tried to force him to enunciate early on the principles for industrial code-making. For months they were on his neck while he was busy with more important problems. How could theories compare with facts? Clearly, a signed, though imperfect code was superior to an unsigned but perfect one. From June until October, 1933, he avoided discussions of policy. And then, one day, he had to face the issue. Secretary Wallace impressed on Mr. Roosevelt that the farmers would not tolerate the proposed 10 percent mark-up provision in the retail food code. The president decided that he had to enlighten the NRA administrator. A handful of impractical professors could be ignored; millions of farmers could not be dismissed out of hand. Theories became facts.

OUT OF THE MOUTHS OF BABES

We waited for him (Benjamin V. Cohen—a leading brain-truster) until we were too hungry to wait any longer. We went in and started to eat. He would doubtless appear shortly. The menu was discouraging; in fact it was close to hopeless. The young man whom we expected would have to be very charming to compensate for his lack of judgment in choosing the restaurant in which we now found ourselves. It had been his suggestion that brought us here.

The entree had just been cleared away, when our latecomer arrived. His refined and intelligent features gave no indication that he would have been so ignorant of restaurants. But then again, all the conscientious employees of the new administration had during the preceding months been working around the clock. He had probably eaten most of his meals at lunch counters or in the office. The introductions had hardly been completed, and the apologies made, when he explained that he would have to run away immediately after dinner. His desk was overflowing.

During the next few minutes the unknown turned into the known. He was a product of the Middle West and had been an honor student at two of America's foremost universities. For the last few months, he had been doing important work for one of the new governmental agencies. He talked easily and well. Of course, one talked all day and all night in Washington: in the morning, one's speeches affected the lives and fortunes of several millions or tens of millions of people; in the evening one talked to amuse one's friends and oneself.

We commenced to argue about the inflationary tendencies of the administration. But the argument was soon transformed into a speech. The young man took great pains to clarify the obvious. "President Roosevelt is confronted with a comparatively easy task; a credit inflation and a large public works program can put a speedy end to the depression. And the President is at this very moment pushing these two approaches: it is perfectly clear that they will succeed." "No!" "Why not? If two or three billion dollars are insufficient, then five will be enough." "No, not even five." "Well, then eight or ten will do the trick." "Of course, there will be no great difficulty in obtaining the necessary funds for the banks will be glad to buy government bonds. And the interest rate will not be bothersome. You have doubtless read Mr. Keynes' *Treatise on Money* and recall how he points out that a negative rate of interest is quite feasible."

Dinner was finished. We said goodnight. As he walked briskly towards his office, I wondered whether he did not occasionally have to pinch himself to remember that he was no longer on a college campus but in Washington. I did.

TRICKS

A high official of the Department of Agriculture came to plead in person. Ten million dollars is a tidy sum but then the ten millions might eventually lead to the expenditure of four billion, surely a substantial amount.

The CWA was allocating funds, and the Department of Agriculture wanted ten million dollars for a census—a very unusual census to be sure. Despite the combined efforts of the best brains in the country, economic recovery had not progressed very far. Farm prices remained low, many factories were working only part time, and the streets were full of the unemployed. Hence, a recovery plan had to be developed which could not fail.

A census was to be taken of all the farms in the United States to discover what articles a farmer would purchase if he had more funds. After the information had been gathered, the government would loan four billion dollars to the farmers, a loan that would run for many years without interest. Clearly, the money would be spent in much the way the census takers had uncovered. Now a concentrated demand for refrigerators, bathtubs, paint, lumber, and the like would lead to industrial prosperity. Agricultural products would then rise in price and the farm community could repay its loan without hardship. (Of course it is none too clear why the census was necessary: it seemed unlikely that the farmers would have refused the loans, or put the money in the bank.)

The representative of the Department of Agriculture was queried as to the government's position if farm prices did not rise, or if they rose and slipped back before the loan was repaid. His answer was to the point: Uncle Sam would have to write off another four billion dollars.

One board member remarked that it was his impression that the present plight of the farmer was in large measure due to his existing heavy burden of debt. How could the Department of Agriculture justify an increase, especially such a large increase. The answer was again to the point: the seriousness of the farm debt problem has been vastly exaggerated; it is really not so bad.

More Tricks

The secretary announced Mr. Joseph Barrows. He was an old but not overfriendly constituent of the senator's. Mr. Barrows had come to say goodbye; he was leaving the day after tomorrow on a six-month cruise that was to take him around the world. The senator was pleasantly surprised by this information for though he knew that his caller was a man of means, he had never placed him in the class of the idle rich. He congratulated Mr. Barrows heartily on his business acumen for clearly in times like these only a very capable businessman could afford such a long vacation. The senator was a little puzzled: how had his visitor made so much money?

For many years, his visitor had been in the habit of leasing Indian lands. It was a large-scale venture, one operated with heavy machinery—plant in the spring, cultivate in the summer, and harvest in the fall. Until the depression, profits had been quite large but during the last years a lessor was fortunate to cover his overhead. This year Mr. Barrows signed a new lease with the Department of the Interior but instead of flying west, he came east. At the Department of Agriculture, he affixed his signature to another contract. The profit from these two conferences enabled him to take the cruise.

The senator was an ardent supporter of the New Deal but when his nonchalant visitor had departed he shouted at his secretary to get the Department of the Interior on the phone. When he was connected he inquired in his most restrained language why the Department of the Interior continued to lease lands when Secretary Wallace was doing his utmost to reduce the amount of acreage under cultivation. The party at the other end asked the senator to please hold on for a very few minutes while he made the necessary inquiries. Soon the voice was heard again: "Section XY 73 of the statutes governing Indian Reservations states that the Secretary of the Interior must lease lands to any financially responsible applicant. Of course, Mr. Senator, if you disapprove, you might convince the members of Congress to change the law. In the meantime we intend to abide by it. Good-day."

FRANKLIN'S DREAM

The king was sad and heavy in spirit. For many days and weeks he had observed the suffering of his people: they were hungry and naked, and yet he was unable to help them. If he could only once again hear the cymbals ring, and see the marketplace full. And then one night he had a dream.

He learned that the citizens of his realm were starving because they did not possess the wherewithal to purchase bread, no less cake. And the little they had today would be still less tomorrow, for their small wages would be further reduced by their almost bankrupt masters. It was only a question of time before everybody would be starving.

The king thought about how he might fill the empty stomachs and clothe the bare backs of his people by increasing their wages. Several of his knights had been anxious to improve the status of their hirelings but clearly they were unable to do so because the majority of their confrères would not follow suit. One did not dare to disregard the wishes and desires of close friends. But the king knew that if his subalterns would act in concord the difficulties that had existed would evaporate. The poor and the humble, the rich and the powerful would all gain by working in concert. True, the knights would have to reduce the hours which their retainers worked; they would have to increase the wages that they paid their retainers; and finally, they would have to add to their staffs. But when they had completed these acts of kindness, and of wisdom, they would reap their rewards. For the land they owned and the products they sold would rise in price. No longer would large estates remain untilled and apples rot because men were too poor to purchase them.

So far, so good. The king was sleeping contentedly. The dream continued. There were dangers in the plan and the kind genie took pains to point them out. It would be foolish for the nobles to lessen the labor of their serfs unless they would at the same time increase their wages. For else, the poor would become still poorer. But the lords would do the right thing: they did not wish to have their apples rot, their wheat become moldy. And the products of the earth could be saved only if the people of the realm were able to purchase them; and they could purchase them only if they had more money. The king was reassured.

But there was one other issue which disturbed the king just a little, like a fly when it tickles the ear of a lion. The nobles must not ask too high a price for the products which they sold, for if that came to pass the poor would be unable to purchase what was available and the rich would see their produce decay under their eyes. The king decided that in the morning he would issue an edict to all the sellers in the country outlawing all price advances, except in those few cases where wages had been substantially increased. For the remainder of the night, the ruler had an undisturbed sleep: his difficulties were at an end.

Daylight brought a change. His staff looked downtrodden and sad; his court was besieged by scores of cantankerous people. Supplicants beseeched him for money so that they would not lose their lands and other possessions. He suggested that they increase the wages they were paying, and enlarge the retinue they were supporting. His chamberlain smiled: the applicants were perplexed. But the king laughed.

Late that afternoon, there arrived at the capital an intimate friend of the king, a man of great wealth and noble character. That evening he dined at court. The king inquired of his friend whether he would be willing to increase the wages of his people if the other knights of the realm did likewise. The guest thought for a moment and then smiled: "Why, yes, My Lord, I should be very happy to do so, if I did not know that my friends could not, and would not, follow my example. They are today, as you know, without funds. But even if they were not short of money, I doubt whether they could be trusted: he who picks his apples most cheaply can sell them most easily."

That night the king slept poorly.

FREE LAND

The frontier is no more, but land can still be had for the asking. Not so long ago, the assistant secretary of agriculture in surveying farming conditions in the northwest, discovered two deep-sea divers who were trying to eke out a living on a farm. They were homesteaders, but he named them deep-sea farmers.

An applicant can obtain a tract of land from the federal government in any one of several western states. True, he does not come into possession of it until he has tenanted it for three to five years. In most cases, the land is good only for grazing; it cannot be farmed to advantage. A wise homesteader therefore attempts to obtain title to the land in the shortest possible time, with an aim of selling his holding to a neighboring rancher. He can seldom afford to buy livestock. Frequently, a wealthy cattle or sheep man will bargain with him: the future owner will build a shack for the homesteader so that the latter can more quickly establish his domicile. The federal government is not very strict.

The choice lands have long ago drifted into private possession. Today, a man can seldom obtain a suitable site. But even with the depressed prices of the last few years, many a homestead can be sold for $1500 to $3000.

PRAIRIE LANDS

Currency manipulation and production control will never solve the farm problems of western Kansas. During the early 1920s thousands of acres of pasture land were ploughed up and for several years the crop yields were excellent. Men made fortunes. But then came dry seasons; the rich soil was no longer rich. Meanwhile erosion was taking its toll. Today, the solution is simple. These lands should be put back into pasture, but no one has as yet been able to find a grass that will seed.

A farmer can be efficient; a bank can be cautious; a government can be helpful, but farmers, bankers and officials cannot cope with an invasion of grasshoppers. When they decide to visit en masse, automobiles are unable to drive without chains. Nor are chains always sufficient. Several years ago drivers in western Nebraska were forced to hang a wet sheet over their radiators: every few miles they took it down, swept off the grasshoppers and were able once again to proceed.

Washington is doing its utmost to help the small farmer save his property and increase his income. That probably explains why the AAA recently sent checks to two farmers in Kansas, one for $25,000, and the other for $28,000.

The president promised to drive the money changers from the temple, and many well-meaning officials sought to put his words into action. But they had only limited success; they were not as able as their opponents. One man on the Mikado's list was especially clever. He knew that the government could employ honest men; he knew that the government could employ intelligent men; but he doubted that the government could employ men who were both honest and intelligent. When he learned that the officials were out for his scalp, he set out for Washington to deflect them.

His deductions were soon proved correct. Before many days had passed, the victim was making suggestions to his judges, and before many more days had passed the judges were acting upon his suggestions. And some dollar bills dropped here and there kept the victim informed of the thoughts and intended actions of the judges.

The wicked knew what the virtuous forgot: there will be money changers as long as there is money!

* * *

Four milling companies, all customers of the same bank ended their fiscal year in the following conditions: one made the largest profits in its entire history, the second lost more money than ever before, the third made a small profit, the fourth broke even.

* * *

A large dairy company deals in the course of a year with 750,000 farmers. The average annual profit of this company has been slightly in excess of $1,000,000. Small wonder that some farmers are interested in sharing in the profits of distributors.

* * *

In one day, a stockyard receives between 8,000 and 40,000 heads of cattle. They must be sold, for it is too expensive to carry them over. The Big Four make the most substantial purchases; one of the four usually buys between 10 percent and 20 percent of the entire market. Now there is good reason to doubt whether the larger companies bid against one another. Why should they—there is a sufficient supply to go around. But still prices do rise.

The adversaries of the New Deal in the Middle West in their efforts to defeat it, have not left many stones unturned. At the time when the cattle control program was under consideration, one heard much of a new governmental agency, the CCTO. Production control was to come about by: C-utting C-ows T-its O-ff.

* * *

During the hectic days when the agricultural refinancing program was getting under way, one of the Federal Land Banks increased the number of its appraisers from twelve to 400. Moreover, under pressure from Washington, loans were made on an expectation of a rise in the value of the collateral. A new era in banking!

* * *

The State of Nebraska has very few miles of concrete roads, but it also has a ridiculously small debt. Constitutional limitations prevent it from exceeding $1,000,000. The state capitol at Lincoln is one of the finest administrative buildings in the country—a skyscraper on the plains—which was built on a pay-as-you-go basis. Every year a few bricks were added.

* * *

Iowa has one of the outstanding highway systems in the United States. One can travel east and west, north and south and never leave concrete. Iowa also floated road bonds in the amount $100,000,000.

* * *

Omaha, Nebraska boasts that it is the fastest growing small city in the United States. This claim might or might not be correct, but Omaha has reason to boast. When every metropolis, and when many smaller cities in the United States were engaged in a wild building boom, Omaha held aloof. Its real estate board prevented the erection of any new commercial or industrial structures; the exceptions were insignificant. Large banks and important corporations were not ashamed to tenant twenty-, thirty-, and forty-year-old buildings.

BAD BLOOD

There was anxiety and tension in the air. The crows seemed to be in a good mood for they knew that hostilities would soon break out—and that meant pleasant pickings. Sullen men in ragged overalls strolled along the highways in groups of two and three casting none too friendly glances at the occasional car that passed. It was hardly pleasant to drive along a principal highway in the second largest state of the union and be unsure whether a case of mistaken identity might not lead to injury or death.

Only a few months previously, the U.S. Secretary of Labor, Francis Perkins, had sought to address the steel workers in Homestead, a town not too distant from the present scene of unrest. She was informed that no one could deliver a public speech without obtaining a license from the mayor. She applied and was informed that "no one could speak in Homestead tonight, not even Jesus Christ himself." The post office was federal property and Madame Secretary commenced to hold her meeting there, but she soon discovered that the workers would not talk freely because of the presence of company spies. After a speedy consultation, the Catholic priest volunteered the use of his vestry building and promised to stand guard at the door to ensure that no one unknown to him would gain admittance. The U.S. Steel Company would have bested the U.S. Government had the latter not received aid from the Church of Rome.

The leaders of labor had not failed to exploit this piece of capitalistic stupidity. Moreover, labor reported that the attorneys for the steel company had had the affrontery to inform the president of the United States that their clients could never deal with an outside union because Mr. Frick had some decades previously written into his will that his mines were never to employ union labor.

Unfortunately conditions are often as perverse as humans are stupid. Over the last cycle, the wages of labor in the captive mines might have been somewhat higher if the stock of U.S. Steel had been somewhat less watered: management would have had more leeway in paying a reasonable wage. But when the mines had been working six days a week, and the mills were running at 80 percent of capacity, there was no real difficulty. It mattered little to a man who received $30.00 a week that his employer could afford to pay him an additional $3 weekly. No blood would flow over such a sum. But when a man worked nine hours for 96 cents and then could work only twice or three times a week, as so many did during 1932 and early in 1933, much blood might flow over $3. But unfortunately, much had happened in the interim. An industry was dying, men were stranded, and profits had been replaced by losses.

And the men did not dare to look the facts in the face. The contemplation of death could offer solace to none. No union could ever restore the bituminous coal fields to prosperity; no union could ever enable the owners of the mines to pay a decent wage; no union could ever increase the average work week from three to six days. The writing on the wall was clear—unemployment, privation, and bankruptcy.

But if one had to die, one could die as a man, not as a serf. And then again, perhaps there was unfathomed strength in labor organization. At least, there would be no more evictions of women in labor and no more shooting of children. But dues had to be paid, pitifully small dues in the abstract, not so small when there was hardly a crust of dry bread in the house. And there were untold nationalities with whom the union officials had to deal—many of the miners understood little English and spoke less. And there were a galaxy of unions fighting more fiercely among themselves than they fought against the common foe. And then there were bitter struggles among the leaders of the same union. It was a mess, a horrible mess. Moreover, the odds were so uneven. The masses lacked everything—ideology, leaders, economic and political power. They knew how to suffer—that was all.

Sullen men in ragged overalls strolled along the highways. They carried guns. The casual tourist sped past, fearful of the hostilities that were certain to erupt. The only question was—when?

First Mate

It was midday and very warm. I felt sorry for the man with a panama hat and no tie and I therefore gave him a lift. I had guessed right. He was no bum—just an unemployed first mate who had left his haven of safety in New York City (the Seaman's Institute where any sailor in good standing can have room and board and even the loan of money until he again finds employment) to apply for a position on a private schooner that was about to be launched from Marblehead. Unfortunately, the idle rich had at last moment decided that the yacht would not go to sea. And here was the ambitious mate stranded some 200 miles from New York.

For twenty years he had been to sea; to all the seas on the face of God's earth. He still wore the silk shirts he had brought for ten and twenty cents during his last trip to the orient. And he still shaved with the Gillettes he had purchased in Central America for a penny. A mate's pay was not bad—room, board, and $180 a month. No wonder he knew life and how to live. But it was not all easy sailing; the government was the bad sister. To take a ship to sea a sailor had to have passed three successive examinations, one at the end of every seven years: To become a master, twenty-one years at sea, a perfect record, a knowledge of geometry and astronomy. And then the responsibility.

He had been on an oil tanker near Tahiti not so long ago when the captain was momentarily unobservant: twenty-two men went down that night, most of them eaten by the sharks before they could reach the rocks; $800,000 lost; and a nine-week trial by a court of admiralty where one is judged by one's peers.

There were stories of the East and of the West, of cargos, rites, and women. And there were discussions about rich and poor, inflations and depressions. But my passenger was not in low spirits. The skipper of the Amberjack II had related to him the prophecy of Mr. Roosevelt which foretold that the country would be in fine condition, some ten months hence (early in 1934).

Here we were in New York. "Well, I'll be home within an hour and a half...little late for supper." "Why, the subway will only take about thirty minutes." "But (and with this his trouser pocket was turned inside out and two pennies became visible) I'll have to walk."

Twenty years at sea...

THE MESSIAH

The president of the corporation (Paul Litchfield, CEO of Goodyear) was thoughtful but obviously perplexed. The company's sales had declined precipitously; competition was increasing daily; the burden of idle plant was serious. Of course, the recent spending policies of the government offered momentary relief. But costs were mounting almost as quickly as profits, and the general outlook remained highly uncertain.

We chatted about economics and economists. And then the president commenced to muse over his college experiences. He recalled his old professor's warning that no man should think himself wise enough to escape from the inscrutable will of economic forces: the laws of supply and demand could not be contravened.

"You know, that old teacher of mine was neither stimulating nor interesting; his lectures were dry as dust. But he did achieve one thing: his students were inoculated against economic romanticism. The training which I received more than thirty years ago was especially helpful after the collapse of '29, for I managed to avoid being taken in by Hoover's pep speeches. Can you imagine what would have happened to this company if it had continued to expand in 1930! We would have been bankrupt long ago. And it's interesting to note that several of the boys who were at college with me, and who today are in control of some of the most important enterprises in the country, have likewise made fewer mistakes than the average run of corporate leaders. Perhaps, the old professor—of course he was not only a teacher but also an excellent executive for under his guidance the college developed into one of the finest scientific institutions in the world—had more effect upon us that I had realized.

"Unfortunately, I have never been able to devote much time to economics but during the past few years I have come to some rather simple and obvious conclusions; and I think that my old teacher would agree with me. Many changes will have to occur before this country really emerges from the depression, but unless I'm entirely mistaken a revision of our immigration policy would be about the most helpful action which we could take.

"Now look, any fool can see that we are suffering from an oversupply of foodstuffs and plant capacity and that these excesses could be easily absorbed if we increased our population by ten to twenty million. Desirable immigrants would not be hard to find; enough people would be willing to migrate from northern Europe, if we only gave them the chance. Nor would there be any difficulty in settling them; the northwest could alone absorb the whole lot.

"We would have more workers and more consumers; and that's what we need. The demands of the masses for a higher standard of living would also be taken care of by large scale immigration, for such demands are always relative, never absolute. A man desires to be better off than his neighbor. Much of the labor unrest would evaporate overnight, if the native population saw ten million new people whose standard of living would be, ipso facto, considerably below their own.

"This approach looks to me to be considerably less romantic than the funny tricks which they are trying in Washington."

THE CEO

One of the executive officers introduced me and I had just sat down when the phone rang. I could not fail to hear what was being said. The state treasurer was begging the president of the company to buy another batch of bonds for the relief burden was mounting and the commonwealth had no funds. Mr. Reffal agreed on the condition that his competitors would promise to purchase an equivalent amount. The transaction was completed within a few seconds. But the exegesis was more interesting than the text. Reffal explained how he really hated to buy any more state bonds but he could not see his way clear to do otherwise. Experience had taught him that it usually paid to be agreeable especially when the state had the power to interfere with the operations of one's business. It was a case of genteel blackmail.

But our CEO had a sense of perspective, a sense of humor. Reffal knew that governments, big and small, were rotten to the core; but he put the blame on big business. Money was the prime corruptor. How could one compare the petty thievery of a state senator or judge to the actions of prominent bankers who were able to make five or ten millions of dollars on a single deal, a deal which was tolerated by the community only because it was secret.

Reffal was well acquainted with the machinery of government. For twenty years he had been forced to devote a substantial part of his time and energy to keeping the state legislature in good spirits, a game he played well. He had balked only once. Some ten years ago, the Ku Klux Klan decided to use crude means to improve the morals of the community—they whipped a woman. Reffal saw red. For the first time in many years, he took a six-month vacation which he devoted to fighting the Klan. No self-respecting male could live in a community where women were whipped. The influence of the Klan began to wane, partly because of Reffal's efforts, partly for other reasons. But the experience of engaging in an open political struggle was not pleasant and he returned to work victorious but chastised. It was easier to make money and buy votes than to buy votes and make money. And the former was more dignified.

In 1928, Reffal cast his ballot for Alfred E. Smith. He was not impressed with the stories that the governor of New York was the illegitimate son of his two principal Jewish advisors, stories which had probably cost Smith many thousands of votes. Reffal's experience with the Klan had taught him that Catholics had no monopoly on bigotry. He, a Protestant, hoped that the American tradition of the separation of church and state could be maintained, but if for any reason that proved impossible, he preferred to go to hell with an educated Jesuit, rather than with an illiterate Baptist or Methodist.

The election of '32 found him on the other side of the fence. It was too dangerous to swap horses in the middle of the stream especially when the current was so powerful, and the shore so close. One need only think of Texas with its oil and wheat, cotton and cattle. An area almost as large as that of France or Germany; and a population only slightly in excess of Paris or Berlin. Yes, people had been despoiling the land for years and probably would continue to do so but Texas was still immensely rich; it could not be impoverished. Of course the depression had wrought changes; it proved that many were not as rich as they once believed. It meant that the daughters of the rich would not be able to trade in their Packard roadsters every year, and their sons-in-law would have to work for a living.

It is nice to have a sense of perspective...

Economists All

The professor of labor defended Mr. Roosevelt. "Why the president is a very shrewd man for he keeps the lid from blowing off, by relieving the pressure whenever it reaches the danger point. This bailing-out policy is indeed very clever.

"The American Federation of Labor has been criticized much too severely. Its craft union philosophy has been the only sensible approach to the problem. And the question of corruption has also been exaggerated. After all, men have stayed out on strike for two years and have starved to death rather than compromise."

The professor of taxation wanted to know why it was not feasible to redistribute wealth through the medium of taxes—if that were the intention of the administration. In the first place one would have to abolish tax-exempt securities. Then, the leakages in the present tax system would have to be stopped. Finally, much higher rates would have to be passed.

The professor of social legislation was impressed with the excellent counselors that Mr. Roosevelt had gathered round him: one need only think of Mellon, Mills, and Morgan to appreciate the change. Moreover, the president is pursuing a wise policy of moderate inflation: once the price level is raised, the debt burden which today strangles the nation's economic life will be greatly eased.

The professor of banking believed that the inflationary policies were doomed to failure and that the dilution of bank assets was a highly dangerous approach. But what could Mr. Roosevelt do? In March of 1933 it was only a question of hours before all of the nation's deposits would have gone up in smoke, The professor of banking admitted that he had sought to reassure the parents of this students that the suspension of specie payments was all for the best. He knew that if the liquidation were permitted to continue, the state would have declared itself insolvent and his salary would have been left unpaid.

Relief

It was January, but the earth was not white. In this part of the country the New Year is ushered in by warm winds and an unfrozen sun, The winter is really more pleasant than the summer for the fields are green and one is not exposed to sunstroke, But winter or summer, men must eat, and men do not eat unless they work. A very few have the good luck to have wealthy parents as a consequence of which they may escape having to work. The Good Lord, however, limits their number to a minimum.

Now Albert Cooke had the misfortune to choose the wrong parents and it therefore became necessary for the state to adopt him. I picked him up at the request of a service station operator who asked whether I would give his friend a lift to the next town. My passenger soon began to talk about his recent past. Before the depression, he had been an automobile mechanic, a trade at which he earned good wages. During the last two years his fortune had gone from bad to worse and when the CWA was formed, he was happy once again to obtain employment. He regretted, however, that he had been forced to take a governmental job: it was a tradition in these parts that no self-respecting man works for the state. Of course, attitudes had begun to change,

Uncle Sam was a pleasant taskmaster; if he were otherwise, Cooke would not be driving around the countryside at 2 p.m. on a Friday afternoon making arrangements with his lady friend whom he was to take to a dance that night. The CWA provided that its employees work a maximum of thirty hours per week, but if they did not reach the limit in any one week, they could make up the lost time within the month.

Cooke had stopped work at noon. During the past two hours, he had made final arrangements with his young lady. And now, he was going to the barber to prepare for the big event. Not only would he have a haircut and a shave, but also a shampoo and a massage. Yes, he could afford it for the government paid good wages. Skilled help received one dollar an hour, thirty hours work per week; and it mattered little, in fact not at all, that the automobile mechanic was now laying bricks. He was a skilled worker.

THE PURE ECONOMISTS

It was Tuesday noon. Fifteen men were filing in for lunch; fifteen directors of personnel of the larger industrial corporations in the city and environs (Rochester, New York). They had been in the habit for a long time of meeting weekly; it was both a pleasant and a useful function. Common problems were discussed and common stories related. The sessions during the past few weeks had been especially significant, for ever since the new administration had commenced to pull rabbits out of the hat substantial citizens were eager to ascertain whether their fellow substantial citizens were as much befuddled as they were. These luncheons had served the useful purpose of reinforcing everyone's belief in his own sanity.

Today's meeting had special significance. The supervisors of the industrial relations departments belonged to nonunion firms; in fact, the city was open-shop, that is all except the needle trades where the unions, even during the depression, had managed to survive. Washington had announced itself in favor of the Forgotten Man, and labor was quick to take the cue. The entire garment industry had been organized with the utmost speed and with a minimum of resistance. Only one diehard remained and he was at this moment engaged neither in the manufacture of suits nor cloaks; he was in the midst of an ugly strike; ugly because the union was determined and strong.

The luncheon progressed but there was tension in the air. One and all, the attendees were oppressed by specters of cancelled invitations and sleepless nights. If their employees should decide to organize their uneasiness would not be unwarranted.

The dessert had been cleared away and the group was now ready to proceed with the business of the week. The chairman, sensing the direction of the unspoken thoughts, decided to make a few remarks about the strike before turning to the program. "These damn foreigners are doubtless responsible for the trouble and let me tell you that unless labor changes its tune and does so quickly, we shall have Hitler and our Nazis on the streets before the end of twelve months." He was about to amplify this statement when he was interrupted by a voice from the other end of the table. The gentleman who demanded attention had no difficulty in securing it, for he inquired in a most mysterious manner whether his colleagues had heard the latest news of the strike. No, they had not. "Well then, it has been proved that this morning the pickets, during an attack upon the scabs, tore the clothing from a woman worker—every stitch of clothing which she had on." Finally, after a prolonged silence during which the industrial relations concillors were assimilating this important bit of sociological data, a porky voice grunted: "There is a time and place for everything." Approval: the meeting proceeds.

2

Big Business

A.P.

The great fire of 1905 impoverished many but it also enriched a few. On the morning after the earthquake, A.P. Gianini was honoring checks and receiving deposits; furthermore, he extended credit. The former produce merchant who had turned to banking some years earlier had once again encountered difficulties. His bank grew but it grew slowly; the financial community did not welcome newcomers. But Gianini's widespread acquaintances among the Italian farmers to the north and to the south of the Golden Gate had given him his start, and the boom which followed the earthquake provided him the opportunity for rapid expansion.

But farmers or no farmers, fire or no fire, Gianini would probably have created a great financial institution. He had a vision, and the vision was of this earth, not of heaven. Branch-banking was known both in Europe and in Canada but it had never been able to make headway in the United States. Now, Gianini knew that if it could once be launched, the advantages would silence the critics forever.

Many years have passed and California now has several large branch banking groups, of which Gianini's is the largest. The country, however, remains antagonistic. When A.P. started slowly to move eastward from the Redwoods towards the Atlantic Ocean, he encountered insurmountable obstacles. Expansion beyond California's borders came only recently. During the first three decades of the century, California provided excellent opportunities for growth. In the late twenties things moved so quickly that whenever a CEO was in doubt as to how to proceed he would form a new corporation. His fellow officers often learned about the new unit only belatedly and sometimes even the founder forgot his creation. But with the boom gaining strength few worried about the complex structure that was being put in place.

In the fall of 1929, the stock market began to behave in a manner unbecoming to stock markets. At first, one hoped, and distinguished statesmen and economists gave one reason to hope, that the market's unbecoming behavior would be short-lived. But as the weeks stretched into months, and the months into years, people lost their faith. Nobody escaped the deflation, the banks least of all.

The Bank of America, into which the Bank of Italy had been transformed when Gianini decided to invade southern California, was particularly vulnerable. Its policies had been shaped in the belief of continued expansion. The large-scale contraction was therefore doubly painful. To make matters worse, early in the depression, A.P. retired and the new management failed to win the wholehearted support of the rank and file employees. The new managers were accused of sabotage and they answered by countercharging insubordination and inefficiency. The nervousness of the public resulted in a decline in deposits to a point where the bank was clearly in danger of collapse. At that point, the A.P. decided to regain control. It was a war for proxies and the employees of the bank found themselves in a strategic position. Not only did they own substantial blocks of shares but they were able to influence the voting of many customers who were also shareholders. Orders came from on high that any employee who failed to vote for management did so at the risk of his job. Although most of the employees favored the return of A.P., they feared for their jobs. They assigned their proxies to the "ins." Shortly before the annual meeting they reassigned them to the "outs." A shrewd lawyer had discovered that a proxy was revocable. A.P. won.

Business conditions did not improve, but the bank slowly began a comeback. The return of Gianini was most important. He had built up a billion dollar institution, and he was the idol of many people. The public knew that the bank had been weakened after his retirement and they believed that it would now revive.

Several days after the famous annual meeting of 1932, a man walked into a southern branch of the bank and inquired of the teller whether it was really true that Gianini was back as head of the bank. The teller confirmed that was in fact the case but the visitor was still unsatisfied.

"Get Mr. Gianini on the phone, I want to talk to him."

"But sir, Mr. Gianini is not in town, he is in San Francisco."

"Well get him on the phone."

"But, I'm sorry, I'm not permitted to make long-distance calls."

"Oh, that's alright—I'll pay for it."

The teller called the home office and within a few minutes Mr. Gianini was on the phone.

"Hello, A.P., is that you? This is John Cornick. I just wanted to confirm that you were back with the bank. Won't hold you up, but I thought you might like to know that I am just making a deposit of seventy-five $1000 bills which I have in my pocket. Hope to see you soon. Good luck and goodbye."

A Banker Remembers

He had risen from the ranks by virtue of his ability and though he was now on top, he continued to keep his eyes open. Moreover, he did not keep his mouth shut.

"Ever since the inception of the Federal Reserve System the personnel of the Board has been a disgrace. I knew them all. With the possible exception of Paul Warburg, they could not even be considered sixth-rate bankers.

"The investment bankers were nothing but the cheapest sort of promoters and don't forget that during the 'twenties almost every commercial bank in the country was in the investment business. It is simply ludicrous for that gang to complain about the Securities Act. Hell, I would have made it more rigid.

"The Federal Reserve Bank in New York has been taking orders these many years from J.P. Morgan and his associates, and the Federal Reserve Board in Washington has in almost every case been willing to follow the advice and suggestions of the New York Bank.

"Without psychoanalysis one cannot commence to appreciate the development of banking in the United States. The presidents of our leading banks, each and every one suffers from megalomania. The insane expansion of the 'twenties can be largely ascribed to this widespread pathologic condition.

"At present the government is blowing off the lid just as it did in 1916–20. The rise in deposits simply reflects governmental spending policies. But my colleagues don't understand; they don't want to understand. It makes them feel so important and so successful to see their assets grow. They can pat themselves on the back and reflect upon their unique abilities."

The Country Banker

He was born on a farm in the Middle West, but he was no midwesterner. His parents had crossed the Rockies while he was still a small boy and today at the age of sixty the last remnants of his Ohio background have disappeared. His adopted region treated him well. True, his schooling had been insufficient, but the lack of a formal education did not stand in his way. Hard work had been well compensated. The poor lad is today the president of a small bank in a small town. At the peak of the boom, his institution had about $2,500,000 in deposits but in the last five years this figure has shrunk by 40 percent. Despite this radical contraction, the bank is in excellent condition; and this feat is due solely to Herbert Rolph.

Throughout the good years, the more prosperous townsfolk implored Mr. Rolph to extend them credit so that they could purchase stocks and bonds and become wealthy. Whenever they were able to present adequate collateral they received the loan, but not before Mr. Rolph had lectured them on the foolishness of their ways. But when the borrowers were unable to provide the collateral, they were sent away emptyhanded. Mr. Rolph would have liked to oblige his friends and acquaintances, but he did not dare.

A good name was good security, but not good enough. Many times during those hectic years, Mr. Rolph had misgivings. The bank was expanding slowly and his own small fortune was increasing at a snail's pace. Moreover, borrowers whom he refused had little difficulty in securing accommodation elsewhere, thereby strengthening his competitors. Upon occasion, Rolph even had doubts whether he was doing the right thing by his family. His friends were becoming wealthier and wealthier but his income and capital showed only modest increases. However, in October 1929, he knew that his instincts had not played him false.

Local industry had never been able to absorb more than a small percentage of the bank's total funds and Rolph had been in the habit of buying commercial paper through a large bank in Spokane. This paper was always very good, and even after the crash, cleaned itself up without any loss. The bond account, though not quite of the same quality, had withstood the storm. Throughout the 'twenties, Mr. Rolph had sought good bonds with high yields; the issue was critical for 50 percent of his deposits were time deposits. From time to time one would have liked to have earned more than 4 percent. The market was flooded with high-yield paper—mortgage bonds of hotels and apartment houses were especially plentiful. But Mr. Rolph had read an article in the *Saturday Evening Post* which pointed out that the vast majority of urban real estate was being financed exclusively with investors' money; the promoters contributed time and energy but not funds. And so Rolph had decided to do without these attractive issues and when they turned into pulp, he did not have to worry.

Five years, five bad years are now at an end but Mr. Rolph is not happy. Commercial paper is almost unobtainable and when it appears it carries a ridiculous rate of 1–1½ percent. Bank deposits are increasing daily and there are no reliable outlets. One must purchase government bonds. But the government bonds create new deposits which help to swell bank deposits still further.

Mr. Rolph is no expert on monetary matters; he does not pretend to understand the ideas of the president's learned advisors. But he does know that more bank failures have occurred because of poor bond holdings than for any other reason. But Mr. Rolph is only a country banker.

BELIEVE IT OR NOT

If inflation ever breaks loose in this country, there will be at least one banker who will know how to act, or how not to act, for he can never forget the lesson he learned some years ago. It was 1923. A young man decided to get married and take a trip around the world. He would sail for the Orient and then work his way westward; Europe would be visited last.

The German mark was acting queerly and had been doing so for some time. The young banker thought that it would be a good idea to deposit some money in Berlin, so that he need not worry about the expenses of the last lap of his trip. In the spring of 1923 he transferred $3000 to the Deutsche Bank which was then paying 8 percent interest on inactive accounts. Then he set sail.

Upon arriving in Tokyo, he was informed that the interest rate in Berlin had been reduced to 6 percent; at Singapore, 4 percent; at Calcutta, 2 percent and at Eden the letter stated that the bank could no longer pay any interest. At Cairo, a note from Berlin informed the newlyweds that a small service charge of 2 percent per month would be levied against all accounts; at Jerusalem, the service charge had been raised to 4 percent; in Constantinople, 8 percent; in Athens, 16 percent; in Bucharest, 32 percent; in Budapest, 64 percent and in Vienna, the provident banker was asked to remit $18, upon the receipt of which his account would be considered closed.

A Sheep Rancher

We arrived at the ranch at lambing time. The hands were returning from the hills with ewes and lambs which they transported in traps not unlike the racing chariots of old. A large barn that had been subdivided into several hundred pens served as the receiving station. The ewe and her offspring usually spent two to three days by themselves; then, they were forced to mingle with the others in the sheepfold; at the end of the week, they were sent to pasture.

Mr. Smith and his helpers were very rushed; so many things had to be attended to at the same time. The ranch was undermanned, but Smith had been hesitant in view of the uncertain market, to increase his overhead. If the ewe were discovered shortly after lambing, one's losses could be substantially reduced. Furthermore, autopsies had to be performed on all the newborn who failed to survive; a disease, if it made headway, could prove devastating. And the newborn that died had to be carefully skinned, and its skin slipped on the bunis (orphaned lambs) so that a childless ewe could be deceived.

Sheep lamb within a few days of one another, and hence the facilities had to meet the peak load. Smith's ranch was well equipped, for Smith was both capable and well-to do. At one time he had carried too much overhead, but his friends at State College had managed to convince him of this fact, and today his ranch was really efficiently operated.

But Smith was skeptical of my friends—and his friends—the "Profs." Introductions had hardly been completed when he ridiculed their advice about keeping careful cost records. True, figures had once proved to him that he could get along with less machinery, and he had saved some money by the discovery, but after all that had been a rather blatant case. Costs mean nothing unless price levels remain more or less stable, and when do lamb and wool prices remain stable? These scientific ideas about ranching are almost as impractical as the recent Washington maneuvers about how to reflate the economy.

"Why, only this afternoon, you have seen the best proof of the insanity of the reduction program. Did I not try to save every single lamb and ewe; you bet your life, I did. You can't suddenly go against training of fifty years and try to prove to a man who has always been striving to increase his yield, that the less efficient he is, the wealthier he'll become. No, it just doesn't make sense. Hell, I know something about this here depression. Last year I read in the paper that there were a lot of people in Chicago who were not getting enough to eat. I had some ewes which were on in years, and I figured that I would sell them for freight so that some poor devils at the other end could get a square meal. Do you know that the ewes never got to Chicago because they couldn't pay their own freight!

"Now, take these farmers here round. I haven't any pity with them. Hell, most of them got into trouble by speculating in land: went and bought farms on the installment basis—paid 5-10 percent cash. They didn't buy to settle; they bought so sell at a quick profit. Sure stood to reason that the thing had to crack, and when it did the whole gang were going to crack with it.

"You can't handle a situation like that from Washington; won't work. How can general principles work when everyone's got a different problem. Look: I'm sheep poor, the next fellow is land poor, the next fellow is machinery poor, and the next fellow is all poor. Just doesn't make any sense to try to average everything out, can't average out these differences.

"Of course the real reason we're in this mess is speculation and tariffs. If we ever get down to earth again, and start to trade with Europe and the rest of the world, we'll have a chance to turn things around, not before. Now, don't tell me that if the country followed my idea, the first thing that would happen would be to remove the tariff on wool. That's O.K. by me if you remove all the other damn tariffs. There's no reason for the government to guarantee me a living. I'll find something to do. And don't tell me that I got brains and guts, and the other fellows ain't, and therefore Roosevelt got to do something for them. Maybe it's so and maybe in ain't. But what you going to do, turn this country into a kindergarten for backward kids?"

Contrasts

Butte, Montana is one of the richest towns on the face of the earth but its wealth is all beneath the surface. During the last fifty years, hundreds of millions of dollars have been taken out of the mines and there is a strong possibility that in the years to come many more millions will be brought to the top.

The depression blighted Butte; Anaconda tried hard to see to it that the townsfolk could continue to work and eat but economic conditions prevented it from succeeding. At the beginning of 1933, an impasse was slowly approaching. The ranchers in the vicinity commenced to string bob-wire around their pastures, and fortify themselves for they feared that the populace would soon take the cattle and the sheep which they could not afford to purchase.

There is no state in the Union which is so completely dominated by one corporation. The press, the schools and the legislature all attest to this fact. A wise man thinks twice before he talks freely. And yet, Thomas Walsh was elected to the U.S. Senate by the people of Montana, not only elected but reelected.

THE PRESIDENT OBEYS

"His visit was announced six weeks in advance, and a month before his arrival we were visited by a member of the Secret Service. The agent wanted to know everything, absolutely everything. We supplied him with blueprints of the properties and the mines, with the names of our more suspicious employees—as if we would have many of them—with a list of all the unsavory locales in and around town: in short we told him what he wanted to know. But that was only the beginning of our trouble. For the next thirty days, our entire organization was upset. The first inspector was joined by other inspectors and as the day drew near, the town was flooded by police. And every day we were put through the same catechism, and every day we were forced to cover the route which the president was to take.

"Finally, the moment arrived. The president was traveling west at great speed and he had decided to spend two hours with us, indeed a great compliment. The drive from the station to the plant proceeded without disturbance; the crowd was jubilant and the president was in excellent spirits. The reception went off like clockwork, and the inspection of the overhead units was likewise a great success. But the president was primarily interested in going underground; he had never been in a mine. The minutes were passing rapidly; one would have to hurry.

"I have forgotten to tell you about the precautions which we had been forced to take. The Secret Service men insisted that there be a foreman and a laborer stationed at every level of the shaft. We really did not have enough foremen, but orders were orders. After all, the president of the United States doesn't call very often.

"The president's car drove to the entrance of the mine and stopped. The Secret Service men did not move, and the president became impatient. A man who was sitting next to the chauffeur and who was obviously in charge, turned his head and murmured a few words. The president clearly disagreed. Once again the agent turned around and this time his words were audible: 'Sorry Mr. President but it just can't be arranged—you can't go.' Mr. Harding looked black, he was very much annoyed. In fact, he reminded one of a child who had been promised a favor and then was disappointed. The officials of the company stood still and looked foolish. For several minutes words flew back and forth. Finally Mr. Harding jumped from his seat and tried to open the door of the car. At that moment the Secret Service man turned for the last time and said: 'Mr. President, you cannot go, I won't *permit* it.' A lady's hand tugged at the president's arm: 'Warren, perhaps you had better not go.' The president's car returned to the station."

KNOWLEDGE VS. FAITH

In September 1928, this savvy businessman (Donald Nelson, vice president of merchandising for Sears Roebuck) sold every piece of stock he owned; and he owned many. He felt certain that the wild stock market had practically spent itself; his friends were, however, firmly convinced that he, rather than the market, was close to collapse.

December came and there was no break, but the cautious businessman pointed out that he made no claims to prophecy; he could not exactly call the day of the turn. His friends were becoming increasingly disturbed by his state of mind. March, and still a rising market. Perhaps his fears were unwarranted: perhaps this was really a new era. No, it could not be, it made no sense; why, look at the condition of the banks. July, my God, could he be insane and his many friends normal? After all, his sanity had already cost him a great many dollars. Everything is relative: the people who are confined to mental hospitals consider those on the outside to be unbalanced.

The pressure was intolerable. The savvy businessman lost faith in himself. He reentered the market with great eclat in early August and was wiped out two months later.

DAVID AND GOLIATH

Towards the end of the last century, the lumber industry on the West Coast got its start. For many years it boomed; men made millions. Prices continued their upward surge until the end of the World War I, and throughout these years, the price for timber soared. But ever since 1920, the trend has been reversed and today most lumberman are land-poor; they have not made a nickel in years.

The Northwest is sparsely settled; Oregon has a population of one million, half of which is centered in and around the city of Portland. The backwoods are wild. Only an occasional settler can be found. Many a Yankee came west after his farm had become infertile or a Missourian pushed over the Rockies to avoid military service during the Civil War. The descendants of these frontiersmen need schools for their children. Naturally the timber merchants must pay the taxes. The community can collect taxes only before the trees are felled.

The legislature has been obliging in carving out school districts according to requested specifications; and the lumbermen have been too loosely organized to defend themselves effectively. Moreover, during the good years, they did not object to paying taxes, even high taxes.

Not so long ago, one ingenious farmer arranged that the boundaries of his school district should be drawn so as to enable him to tax timber sixty miles distant. His home was on a river and he managed to have the school built on the opposite shore. As president of the local school board he appointed himself ferryman. Every morning and every afternoon he transported the children to and from school; the total attendance was two— his own son and daughter. In addition to ferryman, he was also janitor. Moreover, he supplied the school with fuel. The teacher was boarded at his house.

FIRE AND SMOKE

The morning was very dry; the moisture had been dropping for days. The fire warden thought that he had better make rounds to check that all operations were down. Of course, only a foolish person would log on a day like this, but the world was full of foolish persons.

He reached one camp about ten in the morning and to his horror discovered that they were operating; he forced them to cease immediately.

Then he set out for a neighboring establishment which he suspected might be working in the woods. And his suspicion proved correct. Shortly before he arrived, a large tree was being dragged over the ground; sparks flew around; soon flames followed.

The wind was blowing and the trees were very dry. Within a few minutes the fire was beyond control. The wind carried the flames form tree top to tree top; the fire could not be fought on the ground. Retreat alone was possible.

Within twenty-four hours 12,000,000 feet of the choicest lumber in the United States had been burnt. It was two weeks and more before the fire was finally extinguished, largely by the moisture that rolled in from the sea. The intense heat probably led to the counteraction. The major damage was done during the first few hours. The smoke pall rose 40,000 feet into the air. For several weeks, eastern Oregon could not see the sun, and even the natives of western Montana, a thousand miles distant, knew that a great fire had occurred.

The burn equalled the total lumber consumption of the United States for the year 1933. But there can be no firm estimate of the loss, until the salvage operation is completed. It is a race between the mills and the beetles. The quarter of a million acres of fire-killed trees can continue to stand for many years; in fact their hard wood would probably remain good for most of a century. But if the long, white beetles invade the woods, the giant trees are doomed. If...

It Never Happens

Men were nailing small pieces of board together; they were working rapidly but deliberately. Odds and ends were assembled into larger units; finally the body emerged. The upholstery was nailed in; knick-knacks were added. The first coat of paint was applied. Wires were connected; the dashboard was nailed into place; more painting.

On a lower level, the frame was being put together. Gears were inserted; the motor was put into position; the rear-end was installed. Each man had a small but specific job. The conveyer belt moved rapidly; no one could dally. The vast majority of the operations were simple, but the pace was deadening.

Careful scheduling permitted different models to follow one behind the other; the necessary parts were near at hand. When the body was completed, and the frame had likewise been put together, the body from above was lowered on the frame below. The synchronization was startling. Both units arrived at the same moment, at the same place. My guide assured me that a mixup almost never occurred; a mistake was very costly. The words were barely out of his mouth when the whistle blew. A body for a small coupe was dangling in midair: it was ready to descend; but another whistle blew and one noticed that a truck frame waited below.

Three hundred and fifty cars are produced in a day; more than forty an hour. An occasional mistake, even a frequent mistake is not surprising. Less than two thousand men are able to handle the line.

Orchids

The president and his advisors, and many other worthy people are no end perplexed by the continued stagnation of the U.S. economy. Several students have assumed that perhaps the devil himself is to blame. But the continuance of the depression is really not as astonishing as the longevity of the prior expansion.

The aggressiveness of the American businessman is proverbial, though recent testimony before the Senate committee that investigated the munitions industry, forces one to have great respect as well for the salesmen of selected foreign countries. But the blue ribbon for successful advertising remains in the United States, for the record established during the twenties has probably never been equalled, no less beaten.

Several years ago, a large corporation headquartered in the West was interested in securing certain contracts. It hired a yacht and decided to entertain the purchasing agents at sea. Now the sea without mermaids could prove boring; the company provided. But mermaids with clothes could prove boring; the company provided. But mermaids without clothes might catch cold; the company provided—an orchid and a hundred dollar bill.

The Service Station

In 1906 the Standard Oil Company of California and the Associated Oil Company dominated the West Coast. In those days garages sold gasoline to the public; they were the exclusive distributing agents. The average spread between the price at which they bought and the price at which they sold was 9 cents a gallon; the retail price was approximately 25 cents.

In the city of Seattle the market was divided between the two large companies and the Standard Oil controlled about 80 percent of the total. Garages bought their supplies on a yearly contract. Now, a bright salesman of the Associated, quietly underbid the Standard price by one cent and soon signed up every garage in the city. One morning, Standard discovered that it no longer had any business. The following day, the newspapers carried a large advertisement stating that the Standard Oil Company would sell gasoline directly from its substation to the public at the wholesale price: (16 cents, plus 2 cents for distribution expenses). The garages were desperate. Here was gasoline seven cents below the market price. They came in repentant mood to the Standard and promised to be good, if only they were permitted to live.

Seven years passed before the first service station was opened. The Standard Oil Company delayed for it feared to lose its garage business.

3

The University

MISTAKEN IDENTITY

I had been sitting quietly sipping a highball and listening to the sad tale of a bright young man who found it necessary to earn his living by teaching at a university thousands of miles from the centers of civilization. After the first few weeks he had exhausted his colleagues and having become acquainted with their approach to life, he hesitated to discuss anything further with them. Only a masochist could enjoy having his earlier deductions constantly confirmed. The students were almost as unexciting as the staff, for the majority attended college not of their own volition, but in deference to their parent's wishes. Rumors had penetrated to the towns and hamlets from which they hailed, that life at college was really O.K.: work was easy and the girls attractive. Many of the students came from homes where the library consisted of one book—an old, leatherbound Bible. A handful of Jewish students created the only ruffle upon the general calm, but unfortunately instead of goading their nordic associates to work, they sank to the general level.

The whiskey was hardly strong enough to check the depressing influence of these depressing facts. Had the recital continued much longer, gloom and despair would have been firmly entrenched for the remainder of the evening. Fortunately, the setting was disturbed by the ringing of the door bell. A youngish man rushed in; he was obviously slightly agitated, for his hair was flying out in all directions. His voice betrayed him.

"Have you got dice?"

"Why, I don't think so, but I'll look."

"Oh, I'm rather certain that you have, for, I think I've seen dice here."

"Well then I'll scurry 'round."

"Sorry old man, don't seem to have dice in the house."

"Gosh, that's tough; I really need dice."

"Hell, why the great necessity?"

"Well, the damn class meets at nine, and I just won't be able to prepare my lecture without it."

"My God, what *do* you want?"

"Why, dice, you know, the darn book—*Investments and Securities* by Joseph Dice."

"Heavens! Dice!!"

ENFANT TERRIBLE

They arrived shortly before noon (University of Michigan, Ann Arbor). Now the odds were against their meeting anybody, for the majority of the staff never came to their offices on Saturday morning, and those who occasionally dropped around would not stay this late. But the visitors were pleasantly surprised. The door at the head of the rickety old stairs stood ajar—somebody was in. The young man knocked and the absorbed reader raised his head and jumped up. Once the mumbling of names had been completed, the young man pulled a letter out of his pocket, and handed it to his new acquaintance, who proceeded to read it with increasing interest.

Professor Copeland had not seen his old friend and former colleague, Carter Goodrich, since he relocated to Columbia several years ago and he was therefore very pleased to have news of him. He could not refrain from belaboring young Ginzberg with a large number of questions. He was still talking of Goodrich when he reread the letter and smiled, "It seems as if this note is meant for the gang—why I'll run and see if Sharfman or Handman are in their offices. Incidently, what's this about a strange book (*The House of Adam Smith*) that you have just written? It seems that Goodrich is rather impressed with it. Well, more anon."

Copeland was back almost before he left with the report that Handman wasn't around, but that Sharfman would be up in a second. The young lady sneezed and suddenly, Copeland realized that she was in the room. He had failed to pay any attention to her; in fact he had failed to catch her name. Rather an interesting looking, really an attractive-looking young lady—beautiful blond hair and bright blue eyes. Copeland was beginning to speculate when the door opened and in walked Sharfman. Introductions anew, and this time he caught her name, Miss Walters. Sharfman commenced to read Goodrich's letter; he read it carefully for he felt that it was especially addressed to him: after all, he was the head of the economics department. Ginzberg and Copeland were conversing in low tones; Miss Walters had gone back to her examination of the books that lined the walls. Sharfman finished the two pages; he was about to enter into the conversation when he noticed Miss Walters: he began to speculate but Copeland cut him short.

"Look here, Sharfman, Ginzberg has just been telling me of his recent work in Washington and in the Middle West. Might get a pointer or two for your speech this noon; he sure seems to have his doubts about plenty of things."

"I surely have my doubts. I've been seeing too much of the NRA in action to be very optimistic about the results. All very nice to increase wages—though I doubt how much they have really been increased—but who is going to be able to buy at the higher prices. Looks to me as if the government will have to dole out lots of money to keep the thing moving."

"I don't suppose that you prefer Mr. Hoover's approach. Probably, Washington has overstepped itself in one or two places but there's surely no denying, is there, that the underlying situation is very much better since Roosevelt came to power? And we economists ought to be mighty happy: not only will our theories be tried out, but we may even get a chance to run the machine. God, we've been waiting for that all our lives."

"I can well appreciate your reactions, Professor Sharfman, and I would feel the same if I really saw any chance of the New Deal experiment succeeding. But frankly, where's the money to come from? Oh, sure, this is a rich country, but that doesn't mean that it can't go bankrupt. We're expanding now based on the anticipation of higher costs. Doesn't look very stable to me, not from what I've seen."

"Too bad, Ginzberg, that we can't really discuss the problem at length—there are a few points that I should like to talk over, but we shall have to leave in a few minutes for this meeting that I'm to address. Oh, here are the women now."

At that moment in walked the ladies. Introductions again. Then the discussion between the men continued with Mrs. Sharfman listening in; Mrs. Copeland and Miss Walters chatted in the corner. Ginzberg was holding forth. He cited one example after another, all based upon his field work, to prove the hopelessness of the Washington experiment. Sharfman and Copeland did not have a chance to answer back: the attack was too sudden, and they were unprepared. However, they could not help but think that perhaps their newspaper reports were a little optimistic; probably, the kid was much too pessimistic. Sharfman looked at his watch. It was time to leave.

"Well, you'll have to come and pay us a real visit. How about running out on Monday for the meeting of the seminar. Come early and we shall be able to chat."

Ginzberg smiled when he remembered Goodrich's description of his former colleagues. Goodrich reported that Handman was by far the most brilliant and the most interesting; Sharfman was courteous and proper though not exciting; Copeland was recognized as an able person in his field and quite a regular fellow.

"If you would walk over to the Commons with us, I think that you could meet Handman; he is coming straight from his home to the luncheon."

The men walked together and the women walked together. It was a short stroll. Sure enough, Handman was in the lobby. He had an intelligent and sympathetic face, and though he was distinctly middle aged, his good looks had not yet disappeared. Sharfman introduced Ginzberg to Handman and then moved on after having expressed the hope of seeing him again on Monday evening. Handman was interested to receive regards from Goodrich, and he was also interested to learn of young Ginzberg's new book. The title and the thesis caught his fancy; but there was no time for discussion; the gong rang.

Sunday noon, Ginzberg received a phone call from Sharfman; the wires were crossed but the message was intelligible. Sharfman wanted to know whether Ginzberg would be willing to take over the seminar for Monday evening? Would he also come early and have dinner with the faculty? Both questions were answered in the affirmative.

Monday, at four, Ginzberg knocked at Sharfman's door. During the first few minutes, conversation was general. Then Sharfman asked about Ginzberg's book. For the next hour, he was forced to listen to an unusual assortment of heresies. Now, Sharfman never considered himself very orthodox but long years at a state university and long years as an administrative officer had taught him the dangers of nonconformity. He was therefore startled at the nonchalance with which Ginzberg demolished accepted beliefs. He marveled further at how Goodrich and the faculty back east could have been willing to be associated, even loosely associated, with such a work. The critics would attack *them*; not an unknown youngster. Sharfman was slowly beginning to believe that he had made a mistake in inviting Ginzberg. He was about to inquire of the subject for tonight's lecture, when there was a knock on the door. In walked Miss Walters. Sharfman was nonplussed. Ginzberg had failed to mention that she had come along, and anyway what was she doing in these parts? Moreover, what was her name? And what was the connection? Mrs. Sharfman had reported that she was a native of these parts. But Ginzberg had been here for only a few days. And he mentioned that it was his first trip west.

"Good afternoon, Miss,—er—er—"

"Walters!"

"Why yes how foolish of me to have forgotten; frankly I didn't forget, I was just a little startled. You know Ginzberg here, failed to mention that you had come along."

"Oh, I hope I'm not intruding."

"No, not at all."

"Professor Sharfman, I think that I'll run up and see if Handman is around; I should like to see him. May I leave Miss Walters here?"

Miss Walters sat down and Ginzberg left. Soon Sharfman noticed that the atmosphere was less strained. The young lady answered the question uppermost in his mind and she did not even have to be asked. Why, Ginzberg was an intimate friend of a friend of hers and the latter had suggested that he look her up.

Upstairs, Handman and Ginzberg were having a fine time. Handman was a European by birth and cosmopolitan by choice, and upon occasion provincial America proved to be something of a strain. And here was Ginzberg, a native of New York, who had studied abroad and who was really more European than American. Handman recognized that he could talk, and what is more, could be understood.

He was slowly coming out of his straitjacket, it had been so very long since last he had unburdened himself, when in walked Miss Walters and Sharfman. Handman was annoyed and then pleased; annoyed that he was interrupted, pleased by the cause of the interruption. Sharfman, watch in hand, announced that it was time to stroll over to dinner; the others would probably be there. Suddenly, he realized that something was amiss: Handman was much too silent. Why yes, perhaps Handman had not had the pleasure of meeting Miss Walters: Sharfman hastened to introduce them.

In walking across the campus, Ginzberg was paired with Sharfman, and Handman with Miss Walters. The head of the department was much quieter; the soothing influence of the other sex had brought his blood pressure back to normal. But Handman gave every indication of reacting in the opposite manner: his voice and laugh became louder and more excited. But soon all was quiet again; the party had reached the commons where the other members of the faculty were waiting. After the introductions had been completed, the group, now numbering about twelve, sat down to dinner.

The food, like most institutional food was wholesome and tasteless; liquor was conspicuous by its absence. Sharfman did his best to maneuver the conversation into general channels but his success was limited. Economics and politics would constantly surface. Often the subjects were not handled with humor or finesse and the discussion became trying. Ginzberg decided to help his host. He suggested to the company that "economists are really little better than racketeers: they receive an income without engaging in productive work. Perhaps economics is not a discipline, and if it is, it cannot be taught. The state legislature is appropriating monies for a hopeless venture." The guests looked solemn, all except Handman. At the very first opportunity, he jumped in and from then on the proceedings became increasingly lively. His biting but good-natured remarks cut right and left; nobody and nothing escaped. One or two of his colleagues became a little restless, for Handman's humor was so close to the tragic. But Miss Walters was obviously pleased, and that encouraged Handman to continue. In fact he could not be stopped. The notes of dissent became more audible, but he continued. Finally, Sharfman decided that things had gone far enough. He interrupted and inquired of Ginzberg as to the subject of his lecture; Handman was silenced. Slowly, the title became clear: "The New Deal, Sense or Nonsense." Sharfman shifted his chair, one or two of his colleagues started to cough, but Handman was quiet.

The chairman became increasingly convinced that he had made a mistake. Miss Walters had helped him to forget the wild statements of this afternoon, but he remembered she was not the speaker. Only a few minutes ago, Ginzberg had called economists racketeers, and only a few minutes hence, he would probably apply equally unflattering terms to the administration. Sharfman hoped that not too many outsiders would be present; his predicament was already sufficiently difficult.

It was time to go upstairs; the seminar had a reputation for starting punctually. The attendance this evening was large: thirty-five or forty students, several faculty wives, and a liberal sprinkling of visitors. Sharfman regretted that the weather was pleasant. Well, he would have to go through with it as best he could.

His introductory remarks were few and general. Sharfman pointed out that the arranged program had been superceded in order that the seminar members might have the benefit of listening to a visitor who was making first hand studies of the NRA. He concluded with the cryptic phrase that whatever Mr. Ginzberg related would doubtless prove interesting.

Ginzberg began by pointing out that the gracious chairman had failed to mention the title of his discourse, which he now took the liberty of disclosing; "The New Deal, Sense or Nonsense." The word nonsense caught everybody's attention and for the next fifty minutes many members of the seminar were unable to keep quiet. Ginzberg gave them cause to be restless. His staccato, didactic sentences were highly critical of the administration and its actions. His evidence was impressive and plentiful. Moreover, it sounded reliable; the chap seemed to know what he was talking about. But, there was no compulsion to agree with his conclusions. True he sounded convincing when he emphasized that either the New Deal would have to be scrapped—hourly wage rates would have to fall, price protection would have to be abandoned, Public Works Administration (PWA) expenditures curtailed or else inflation would be inevitable.

In concluding, he sketched the possible social and political implications of national bankruptcy: economic stagnation, fascism, racial outbreaks. But his humor did not desert him. He pointed out that he could not lose: if his analysis were proved to be wrong, the country would prosper and he would be happy; if his analyses proved correct, the country would suffer but he would have the intellectual satisfaction of having been an early prophet. The audience could guess which outcome would please him most.

The performance was at an end and Sharfman alone seemed to regret the fact; he dreaded the moment when he would have to close the meeting. But first, there were a few questions. The points raised were often wide of the mark, and Ginzberg was not gentle with his answers. His biting replies silenced the timid and soon the questions were over. Now it was Sharfman's turn. He knew that he dare not be lavish in his praise for the morning newspapers would probably cause him enough trouble by reporting the speech; on the other hand, he had been instrumental in inviting Ginzberg. He met the dilemma perfectly; twenty years of academic life had not failed to teach him a trick or two. The chairman reminded the seminar that his opening remarks had been proved correct; the lecture had been interesting, most interesting. The audience clapped. Handman and Miss Walters smiled.

Ten minutes later, Sharfman arrived home. He took a long drink and then sat down to write his former colleague, Carter Goodrich, a short note.

Faux Pas

The committee had originally invited the president to dine with it, but for one reason or another the president suggested that the several professors come to his house for dinner. It was of course a formal function.

Walter Retlaw came a few minutes early. The several pictures and etchings decorating the walls caught his fancy. His attention was especially arrested by a cleric with a long beard and skull cap—the face was unusually intellectual. Retlaw could not refrain from inquiring how the rabbi's picture happened to be in the room. His host informed him that it was no rabbi but his old and venerable friend, the Methodist bishop of the Southwest. Silence!

Somewhat later in the evening the host was attempting to explain the difficulties that beset an administrator. Ideals were fine, but realities were stern. He illustrated his point by referring to Jesus, who despite his gospel of love did not act kindly towards the moneylenders. Retlaw interpreted the story differently. He pointed out that the Gallilian prophet momentarily forgot his principals. Silence!

The dinner was almost at an end, when the conversation began to lag. Retlaw decided to help out. He inquired what his colleagues thought of the new magazine that had just appeared on the campus: it seemed to him to be extremely well written and quite intelligent. No one answered. Suddenly, Retlaw remembered that the last issue carried a scathing attack upon the president. Silence forever!

Trials of Youth

Union House dominated the campus. It was comfortable without being luxurious, practical though attractive. The state legislators had really done very well, but they found little joy in their work. They discovered that they had unwittingly encouraged the desecration of the Sabbath, for it was well known that on the Lord's day, boys and girls lounged around the piazza in beach pyjamas and dressing gowns.

The merchants in town also had their doubts about Union House. During the period of its construction they had collected a fund and outfitted the grill. Today, the attractiveness, convenience, and low prices of the university center were undermining the businesses of many of the benefactors.

From time to time, the state elected a liberal governor and there arose, especially in outlying areas, attacks on the university as a center of liberalism. But the facts did not support the critics. The legislature was seldom as liberal as the chief executive, and it was the legislature that controlled the purse strings and hence controlled the university. The farmers, merchants, lawyers, who sat in the state legislature were never inclined to put substantial funds at the disposal of the university. Salaries were low and the college administration had to work hard to see that they were not lowered. Occasionally, the university sponsored an experiment in education, but if the opposition became too vocal, the administration retreated.

The university officials had learned from experience that it would be impolitic, in fact suicidal to disregard the prejudices of the majority of the citizens. The college could afford to be only one or two steps ahead of them. A truly liberal institution would be permanently estranged from the populace.

The student body was drawn from the small towns and hamlets throughout the state; a substantial minority came from metropolitan centers in the East. The number of boys and girls was about equal, and student discipline presented difficulties. The members of the legislature were strong supporters of Christian morality; they were therefore determined that the young should not be corrupted, at least not corrupted with the monies that the state appropriated.

The Solons made only one mistake: they vastly overestimated the innocence of their own sons and daughters. The majority of the freshmen were well prepared in extracurricular subjects. The out-of-state students were perhaps more radical in thought, but not in action. The young, especially girls, are more restrained in large urban centers than in small rural communities.

Two stories reflect student morality. Tradition has it that the Great Emancipator, whose statue guards College Hall, will arise from his chair when the first virgin passes. A more recent tale relates that a group of boys stole a gravestone which they reset in the front lawn of Alpha Beta Gamma sorority. The inscription read: "To Agnus Grey, the last of the Alpha Beta Gamma virgins, who departed this life in the year of the Lord, 1823."

The legislators have done their utmost to hold the youngsters in check. They even went so far as to prescribe compulsory examinations in every required course: the students must be tested at least once in six weeks. But book learning faces strong competition. For instance, the girls' dormitories are situated on the border of a small forest. Few students can resist the temptation of caring for their bodies as well as for their minds. Hence, they frequently take long walks, especially in the crisp night air. During the day, the classics are frequently neglected for geological investigations; the terrain is most interesting. But even then, many youngsters tire of the out-of-doors and seek refuge in nearby warm, friendly hotels.

The administrators do their utmost to reward the virtuous and punish the wicked. The legislators must not be unsettled. Several months ago, the dean's office was informed that a young man was paying an extended visit to a young lady. The boy was a member of the senior class and one of the outstanding students in the university; the girl was also a superior student. They were engaged. The dean rushed to the apartment and took up his post outside the door. The flat had but one exit. The dean borrowed a rocking chair and waited.

Lucy

We arrived just as dinner had been completed. The guests were moving from the dining into the living room. They had been eight at dinner. Two historians, one philologist, one chemist, and their wives. The host was a member of the history department. (Nothing is so rare as a bachelor professor at a small college; they just do not exist.)

The general drowsiness led one to believe that the dinner had been substantial; for the guests showed no signs of animation; they almost lacked the energy to shake hands with my friend and myself. It did not take many minutes before the assembled company had again rested its weight. The women sat side by side upon the sofa which had the distinction of being the only comfortable piece of furniture in the room; the men found resting places as best they could. The choice lay between homemade chairs and family heirlooms.

After the first few minutes, conversation stagnated; no subject attracted and held attention. It was not long, however, before an undercurrent of tension was noticeable. Here sat ten adults, supposedly educated adults, adults who in fact earned their daily bread and butter through speaking and now they sat like a group of mutes. The children of the house became slightly obstreperous and a minor commotion took place. But it was not very long before the hostess had managed to quell the disturbance and once again silence reigned.

Competition in talk is serious, but not nearly as serious as competition in silence. Some of us tried to break the ice, but our acute awareness only added to the difficulty; the more we strove, the more we failed. Finally the hostess was constrained to take strong action. She suggested to the ladies, in much the tone that a general uses in speaking to second lieutenants, that they withdraw to the other room and play a game of pool on the children's miniature table. The wife of the philologist who looked as dead the thirteenth-century French verbs that her husband studied, demurred faintly: she remarked that she was really inept at games and had never held a pool stick in her hands. Her protestations were in vain. She was shooed off with the others.

The men readjusted their seats. Now that the women had left, there was no reason for them to develop acute backaches. Somebody mentioned England. That started us off. Within a few minutes we were discussing contemporary English literature; Joyce and Lawrence were explored. And then it was Huxley—*Point Counter Point*. All had read it, and all had been impressed, in fact impressed with the same part of the book: *Lucy*! One of the historians talked of his student days in Paris when he had spent more hours in the Montmartre then in the Bibliotheque Nationale. But even he was frank to admit that although Barbette and Marie and the rest had been charming he had never met anyone who could hold a candle to Lucy. What a girl she must have been. One of the group, I think it was the philologist, was so irreverent as to suggest that Lucy was overdrawn, there simply could not be anyone as attractive as she. But Lucy had her defenders that night. We all jumped on our friend and forced him to beat a hasty retreat. There was a great harmony in our thoughts and reflections: one and all, we were thinking, contemplating, evaluating our chances of ever running into Lucy in the flesh. But at that moment our reveries were rudely interrupted.

Four talkative females swooped down upon us. They were most animated. We were forced to listen to a recital of this good shot and that mistake; of one's victories and the other's losses. Not one of us had sufficiently recovered from his reverie to react with even a modicum of politeness. But at that moment, Lucy was banished forever. The hostess served ice water and crackers.

THE CAMPUS

The college is not unimpressive though an ignorant visitor from New York had once marched up the front stairs of a neighboring institution and inquired whether Professor Roberts was in. No, not yet; it was the state penitentiary.

The surrounding country with its long smooth hills and large decorative trees is beautiful most of the year round. The color scheme is superb both in spring and in fall and in winter the snow blankets the area. The college is horribly isolated despite assurances to the contrary of one faculty member who pointed out that the location was ideal. Why, the campus was just 250 miles from this important city; some 325 miles from a center city and only 400 from a major metropolis. The radio programs are so clear; no static whatever. The town itself is very small—some 5000 students, some 2000 employees of the college (professors, instructors, library aides, and caretakers) and once again that many inhabitants who care for the physical needs of this intellectual community. Caring for the needs of the college is an exaggeration. There are but two places to eat—the College Grill and the Corner Store. Privacy is priceless but it is unobtainable. If one desires not to be interrupted while eating, one must drive sixty miles, and then choose between two or three restaurants (formerly an additional one or two speakeasies) in a dirty industrial town. Nor can one be absolutely certain to avoid the familiar, for it still remains the nearest town to the campus. Perhaps, an acquaintance is also trying to escape for an evening.

The married faculty, and the overwhelming proportion are married, have no money to patronize restaurants. The purchase of necessities, the mortgage on the house, and the installment payments on the car hold them prisoners. But lack of money is a minor inconvenience. After the first few years, sometimes even after the first few months, ambition and tastes decline. A visit to the relatives on Easter or Christmas; a few weeks in the country during the warm summer days; an occasional dinner during the academic year are sufficient. Books are seldom purchased—it is not difficult to rent the most recent fiction from the circulating library.

An air of unreality pervades the institution. Here are men whose lives are supposedly dedicated to the advancement of learning and they are almost illiterate. Their adjustment to their work is comparable to a group of violin and piano carpenters—carpenters who play off tune. There exists an almost pathologic preoccupation with sex for what else can stimulate? Moreover, the obvious frigidity of many of the women forces their husbands to be concerned with the problem. No escape exists. The men spend not a few hours a week in teaching and an equal number in playing golf or tennis. Their wives however do nothing but talk. Now, the proclivity to gossip is perhaps universal but interesting gossip without interesting experiences is impossible. Bitterness compensates for variety. The men have no incentive to fight against the poison fangs of petty conversation: time must pass, how else can it be spent? One shudders when they discuss the books they are writing, have been writing for the last ten, fifteen, or twenty years. It is the closet ghost of their student days when they were inspired, at least in some small degree, to study and write.

Some few, especially among the younger men, are hopelessly trapped. In a foolish moment they married. Their upbringing made it impossible for them to satisfy their sexual desires except inside the institutional setting conspired to reinforce the difficulties of any but an orthodox adjustment. And here they are bound hand and foot: a wife, a child or two, many hours of teaching, and a salary of $2000 annually. And time most likely has cooled their passion, but Eros cannot be thrown over: he will exact his payment. They cannot proceed with research because they are untrained; they cannot obtain training at the campus; and they cannot leave.

The average intellectual ability of the faculty can best be estimated by the fact that only the army group (instructors in ROTC) are able to play contract bridge—the majority find the game too difficult. Moreover, the administration has conspired to outlaw any form of intellectualism or at least does nothing to further it. Some twenty and more years ago, a bright young man became a member of the faculty. In the course of time two remarkable things happened: first, he continued with his scientific researches; secondly, he remained on the campus. On the occasion of a rise in salary, the chairman of the board took him aside and impressed upon him that his salary was being increased because of his teaching abilities and emphasized that his unusual success with his classes led the board to overlook his escapades—his writing and publishing of books. Today, the disillusioned man knows that academic isolation was turned into academic insulation. The utmost concentration and devotion to one's work was not sufficient to overcome the lack of intellectual criticism or emotional understanding.

Universities are supposed to be centers of cosmopolitanism; the campus however, seldom interacts with the rest of the cosmos. The mores are decades, almost centuries out of date. For instance, dinner parties begin at six or at the latest six thirty. One eats well but of course there is no liquor. Conversation does not extend beyond the three K's.

At about nine o'clock the party breaks up—at least, for the first time. The gentlemen escort their wives home, and even unmarried women are shooed off to bed. Then the men reassemble at the house of their host. Liquor is poured, cigars are smoked, stories are told. The evening progresses without further disturbances unless the hostess should inadvertently decide to take a bath, a fact which the thin ceilings and partitions cannot hide. The risque stories would then lose a little of their appeal for even an unimaginative visitor cannot help but think of the hostess splashing around in her tub.

The students are decidedly superior to the faculty; they have two distinct advantages. They do not have to earn a living and they do not have to support a wife and children. Moreover, a large number actually belong at college; they have intellectual interests and not a few have intellectual gifts. Of course, after two years on campus promising students frequently lose their promise and decide to concentrate on fraternity and school politics. But their youth saves them; no matter how rapidly they deteriorate, they are unable to catch up with the faculty within the short time at their disposal. After all, they are on campus for only four years.

The boys outnumber the girls about six to one and this factor can hardly be overemphasized in evaluating life at campus, especially when one remembers the great isolation of the institution. A young lady who does not suffer from nymphomania is certain to have a husband at the end of her studies, that is if she desires a husband. The more or less psychopathic females can prove their sophistication by sleeping with three or four men during a week. But the number of "modern women" is restricted. Hence, one can see every Saturday evening a bus load or two of men ready to leave for a neighboring town where the hostesses at the dance will assure that nobody is lonely. The bus never fails to return to campus in time for Monday morning's first class.

But the students are really to be pitied. They can spend their evenings going to the movies which incidently, are not cheap for like all prices at campus, movie prices are monopolistic; drinking, also no cheap amusement; or driving around. Many of the students have cars and it is easy to borrow one. But the orthodox and churchy matrons have banned together to patrol the roads and prevent parked cars from having their curtains drawn.

The campus is beautiful but horrible. Unlike its neighbor, the state penitentiary, it houses few real people, mostly ghosts.

Misfit

Ten years ago Herbert Nigor went west to seek his fortune. He knew that he would never be rich, but he hoped that he might be happy. Any change was a change for the better; it would take him still further from the scenes of his youth. Those fifteen years in Europe were a nightmare and his last ten years in the East were not much better. At home, it had been economic and intellectual starvation; in New York, social starvation. But now things would begin to change: a new life, in a new community.

The position was unimportant and the salary meager; but security and time for research were worth much. He had been engaged to teach modern history and if his classes and books found favor, promotions would come.

His reception was not warm; obviously the old fogies were not keen about this new addition to the faculty and they made no effort to hide their reactions. A foreigner was a foreigner either in the East or in the West. And this foreigner had a sharp tongue which cut much too deeply, for it cut cleanly.

The first year passed quietly. His more extravagant hopes evaporated, but the future still promised much. At the beginning of the next academic year, Nigor received a severe blow; the university appointed a new man to a full professorship in his field.

His colleagues were hostile, indifferent, or condescending; a few interesting and grateful students alone made life worthwhile. Nigor's tongue became sharper. He worked on his dissertation, a pioneering study, which his professors in the East recognized to be important but it proceeded slowly.

Years passed. He married, children came. But disappointments continued to mount. At times of promotion, younger and less capable men were advanced. It was impossible to keep quiet; and yet, the more one talked, the more hopeless conditions became. The dissertation was finally completed and Nigor returned east to defend it. Many of the old professors were no more; the examiners were correct but formal. Of course, the work was accepted, but its completion afforded Nigor little pleasure. The faculty in the West could not appreciate it, and the faculty in the East was no longer interested.

The administration offered him an assistant professorship, which he promptly refused. Only an associate professorship could compensate for past slights. But certain members of the faculty were openly antagonistic and the regulations stipulated that the candidate must have published at least one book to be considered for the post of an associate professor. Dissertations didn't count. After all, a dissertation is a dissertation even though in most cases it remains unread, while in a rare instance like the present, it will be recognized as a significant piece of scholarship.

Nigor lost interest in the field; he could not continue to write. He wanted to teach and think. But the pressure was ever present. Books for a professorship or no camp for the children.

His colleagues did not have to worry; they had social and economic security. How he envied and how he despised them: stupid, mediocre men but alas, not strangers!

4

Southwest

BIG HATS

For those of us who were brought up on the movies, the Lone Star State is a great disappointment. One finds little excitement or adventure in the larger cities. For instance, Houston gives the impression of being a model community; one could almost suspect that a group of Brains-Trusters were responsible for its development. However, upon closer inspection the city appears more human, more American. There are two distinct business sections; in fact there are two office buildings for every one that is needed. Several years ago, two wealthy promoters failed to get together, and today, Houston is not unlike its many neighbors.

When one recalls the traditions of the Southwest, real estate speculation can be appreciated, but the police and traffic regulations cannot be readily understood. It is a strange and somewhat upsetting spectacle to watch the giants of the ranches stand on the street corners and wait for the lights to turn. They do not dare to put even one foot into the gutter, for the police are liberal in handing out summonses for jay-walking.

Night life is equally depressing. Slot machines and movies have taken the place of cattle rustling and kidnapping. No longer are beautiful girls terrorized by outlaws; men wait long and patiently to gain admission for a film entitled: *Sins of Sex—For Men Only*.

But one relic of the past is still preserved. An unfinished building is not taxed at its full value. A prominent banker, Jesse Jones, had not plastered the top floor of his building and the full tax rate has never been applied.

PATRIOTISM

No statesman has ever suggested a plan to dismember his country, but upon occasion politicians have advocated the partition of their states.

There has been frequent agitation to divide Texas into four states, a most desirable reorganization when one realizes that it would lead to the creation of a large number of new positions: four governors; four legislatures; eight senators. Every good Southerner should be sympathetic, for the plan if carried out would do much to reestablish a balance of power between North and South in the Senate.

In recent years, the proposal has made little headway and it is extremely unlikely that it will be pushed aggressively in the period that lies ahead. One of the men most interested in its success is now the presiding officer of the Senate and he would probably be disinclined to increase the difficulties of his task.

IDEALS

The descendants of Daniel Boone no longer wage war with the Indians. In fact they no longer even dream of waging war with the Indians. To create wealth is exciting, but to enjoy it is even more exciting. Now the vast majority of the population is more interested in spending than in making money.

After four years of depression Frank Hawkins was still on the payroll of a large corporation. His salary of $3000 was quite large when one considered the low cost of living. But he dreamt of an even brighter future.

"A salary of $25,000 annually would be sufficient; more money would only lead one to worry; a large house in the country; only a foreigner could be satisfied with an apartment: six children or so; a golf course close by; it is ridiculous to drive twenty minutes before one can tee off; and finally, a job which would necessitate neither physical nor mental strain; one wants to work but not too long or too hard."

Perhaps Mr. Marx will yet put Mr. Freud out of business; perhaps not.

THE CYNIC

A political system can survive in one of two ways. Either the vast majority of the population tolerates it or else the bayonets of the government force the population to tolerate it. While Mr. Roosevelt had no intention of using bayonets to help the New Deal, he experimented with forced economic expansion and the public responded. But this policy led to some weird paradoxes.

An important businessman in the South was no end disturbed by a critic of the administration who ventured to express his doubts about the deliberate effort to raise the price level. He would listen to no criticism of an administration that had succeeded in changing the entire business picture: losses had been turned into profits; bankruptcies had given way to expansion. Obviously no praise was too great for the man who had wrought so much good.

Now, unfortunately, Mr. Roosevelt had been unable to prevent fires and as ill luck would have it a conflagration broke out in the refinery of this important business man. The fire raged for many hours and the entire workforce helped to fight it. On the following pay day, the personnel department arranged to compensate the men for the extra hours they had worked. Many were skilled employees, and hence received an average hourly wage of sixty to seventy cents. The personnel department planned to pay them at their regular scale, but Mr. Roosevelt's friend insisted that firefighting was unskilled work, and hence should be paid at the rate of forty cents an hour, not a penny more.

The total sum involved was $500!

CLOTHED IN GLORY

A Northern minister was vacationing in a very rich, but now very depressed section of Texas. The farmers were so short of cash, that they had even been forced to dismiss their pastor. The visitor volunteered to help them out.

At the conclusion of the Sunday morning service, one of the elders invited the kindly clergyman to his home for dinner. The latter was reluctant to accept for he knew of the poverty of these farmers and hence feared that what little he would eat would fail to satisfy him, but would at the same time deprive his hosts of essential nourishment. But he found it impossible to refuse. Upon arriving at the farm, he was no end surprised. The table was ladened with melons, stuffed turkeys, vegetables, sweets, and pies. The pastor ate a hearty meal. When he was about to leave, he could not refrain from remarking upon his original fears. His host smiled in amusement, and then hastened to point out that if the clergyman would return this way next year, he would find the finest collection of fat, naked farmers that he had ever seen.

Oil

Barnum is dead but oil promoters are still very much in the picture. Specialists in gullibility come and go, but the well digger remains forever. During the past few years, his work has been materially reduced for the radio has taken a load from his shoulders.

Today, the search for oil can be conducted with a very few dollars of one's own capital, just enough to launch an advertising campaign. Americans have never been a bookish people; their natural empiricism has led them to trust their senses rather than their intellect. An oil promoter does not lecture those whom he is trying to enrich; nor does he present them with charts and graphs. No, he appeals directly to their horse-sense. Night after night, the radio carries the message of the progress of the drilling: how the level has almost been reached; how barrels will soon be filled with the subterranean fluid. And then, one night, the microphone is connected to the rigging, and soon swishing noises are heard. The oil is coming, but the dollars have come earlier.

Shortly after the opening of the east Texas field crude oil was purchasable for five and even three dollars a barrel. The general chaos, like all chaos in the production of oil is largely the result of the foolish legal dictum, long established, which holds that oil is a fugitive good and therefore belongs to whoever brings it to the surface.

It is customary for a prospector to lease a tract of land at a nominal figure and set out in search of oil. He carries all of the development charges, and if he is so lucky as to make a strike, he retains seven-eighths of the proceeds and pays over one-eighth to the owner of the land. Now it frequently happens that the owner for one of many reasons sells a portion of his claim to future royalties and this claim is then subdivided many times over. The lessee must then apportion the correct percentage of the royalty to each holder of a claim: occasionally, he mails checks for ten dollars and twenty dollars.

Royalty claimants can prove most annoying. For instance, if the lessee is anxious to come to an understanding with other operating units, he must first obtain the consent of each and every royalty owner.

Science has not been able to discover the presence of oil, but it has done much to forecast the absence of oil. The development of geophysics has saved many a prospector large amounts of money, for it is no cheap matter to drill. In former days, the apparatus and the labor cost approximated $50,000; today, these costs have been reduced, but they are still considerable.

MEN VS. BRICKS

Several years ago the state of Texas ceded a large tract of land to the university in the hope that the income therefrom would help to meet a portion of the university's annual budget. The land was of little value, and the income was inconsiderable. One day, oil was discovered. The university was on easy street. Unfortunately, someone reread the grant and discovered a clause which stated that the income could be used only for capital expenditures, not for operating expenses. The university's physical plant was in poor condition, hence the administration was not disheartened. But the gods were in ill humor. The question was raised subsequently whether royalties were capital or income. The court decided that royalties were capital and could therefore not be touched; only the interest on the royalties could be spent.

Despite these extreme restrictions there were sufficient funds available to begin rebuilding the campus. No longer would a lecture on gravitation be interrupted by a professor flushing a nearby toilet; the wooden buildings were to be razed. But instructors might still be exposed to the rain, not on, but off the campus, for their salaries have just been reduced by 30 percent.

THE LONE STAR STATE

Texans typify the American interest in extremes. For instance they are no end impressed with the size of their own state. They love to tell the story of a St. Louis businessman who wrote to his partner in El Paso that he should please run over to Houston and call on his relatives, and received a wire in return: go yourself, you're nearer." Or again, the tale of the man from the Panhandle who used to go once a year to Brownsville: on one such trip, he discovered that Canada was closer to his home than southern Texas.

Distance is not oppressive in Texas: landscape and the atmosphere conspire to deceive the innocent. A motorist frequently plays a game with himself of estimating the number of miles between his present position and the town yonder. If he is not a native and natives for the most part would not play the game, he will discover that his guesses are way off the mark. A town that appears to be but four miles distant—for one can clearly see the smoke rising from the tall stacks—will prove to be twelve to sixteen miles away.

It is a common occurrence for a farmer and his wife to have an early supper, drive eighty miles to spend the evening with friends, and return home before midnight. One hundred and sixty miles for a few rubbers of bridge!

Herbert Roberts was a close friend of the Ferguson children, and one afternoon he ran into one of them on the street. Young Ferguson remarked that Roberts must drop around see the governor. Roberts replied that nothing would please him better for he did want to follow up with the governor a conversation that they had started the other night. Young Ferguson looked perplexed; then he laughed, "Why, I meant that you should come around and see *the* governor, not Ma!" *

During the depression many states and localities devised ingenious schemes for collecting more revenue. But it is doubtful whether a more original method was devised then by the Southwest tax collector who offered a tobacco wholesaler $500.00 worth of tax stamps for $100.00.

Western railroads have managed to decrease their deficits in recent years by transporting car loads of Mexicans back to Mexico. And the more they transported, the more there were to transport. It might have facilitated matters, if the railroads had been permitted to bring back one immigrant for every emigrant. Frequently, Mexicans crossed the border, more quickly on foot than by train.

Gossip has it that these same railroads have been kept fairly busy in early spring and in late fall by cattle movements between Mexico and California. It is not impossible that many of the shipments were made to and from the ranches of a distinguished native son, one who has long been a leader in the Buy-American Campaign.

El Paso is the most westerly outpost for Negroes, the coast cities alone excepted. Now, its Negro population is distinctive for several reasons. In contrast to the whites, most colored folk do not have to live in El Paso;

---

*Miriam A. (Ma) Ferguson was governor of Texas from 1925 to 1927 and from 1933 to 1935.

their health is good. Years ago, the original blacks were imported to break a railroad strike and many have remained to work in the yards to this very day. But a Negro has never had great difficulties in securing employment, for they are more efficient and reliable.

The city has an ideal climate and yet its death rate is the highest of any in the country. Almost every white man or woman suffers from a pulmonary disorder or else is the close relative of a sufferer. Sick folk have come to El Paso from the far corners of the country, for the size of the city enables them, especially if they are not very ill, to engage in business and lead a normal life.

The Mexican population is approximately equal to the American, but there is little intercourse between the two. Nor do the Negroes mingle freely with the immigrants. In fact, blacks have very little use for Villa's descendants.

BUREAUCRACY

Juarez is a town of which I know very little, for I had the bad fortune to reach the border just as a small epidemic was beginning to crest. Twenty or more deaths were known to the American immigration officials who doubtless had not gone out of their way to verify the statistics.

If codes of fair competition were ever to be drawn to cover both sides of an international border, the American officials at El Paso would be restrained from engaging in practices they now follow. Of course one would have to make the naive assumption that international courts would be less derelict in the pursuit of their duties than national courts.

The American tourist who approaches the bridge that leads to Mexico is usually in a state of excitement. Many have never before left the United States and the visit to Mexico is therefore an exciting event. Hollywood had prepared him: wine, women and song. But alas if he stops to chat with the American officials his elation will not last long. The officers warn him not to leave the main street; that he should go no further than the square; that he should be most circumspect and at all possible costs avoid altercations. And if the downcast tourist gives the least indication that he appreciates the information his education will continue. He will be told that the town is unspeakably dirty, that the women are fat and ugly, that the liquor is poor and expensive, and that Juarez is really the last place in the world that one should visit.

If he should have the good luck to reach the border at the time of an epidemic, he will be subject to further indoctrination. He will be told in no uncertain language that he may expose himself to the pest but he should not imagine that the folks back home will be permitted to share his foreign experiences. No, he cannot reenter the United States without being vaccinated. The more cautious and timorous sightseers are by this time willing to beat a polite retreat.

But the excursion to Mexico is not yet at an end. During the preceding minutes the health officials connected with the department of immigration have probably worked themselves into the visitor's circle of consciousness. And now it is their turn. They advise the disillusioned traveler to be vaccinated even though he has definitely given up the idea of visiting Mexico. After all, it is a simple procedure: a scratch with the needle, the injection of a bit of liquid, and a swab of alcohol. If the prospective victim begins to squirm, but fails to accept the offer, the officials attempt to break his resistance. They point out that the epidemic has not been completely controlled; there have been isolated deaths on the American side of the border: the constant movement of men and goods made this inevitable. Further a person who has spent even a moment in the customs house, not to mention half an hour, is practically in as great a danger as a visitor to Juarez, for people from the pest ridden city are constantly passing through the turnstiles.

Some days later, a tourist at the Grand Canyon suddenly has a mirage of Mexico. His arm pains him so greatly from a post-vaccine reaction that he can do little else but concentrate on the one Spanish word with which he is acquainted—*manana*.

Several hundred miles distant, another tourist is maneuvering his way through the subterranean passages of the largest caves in the United States. He has been walking for several hours with stooped head and bent knees. Suddenly he begins to feel ill; chilly and feverish. At that moment he remembers Juarez, the black smallpox epidemic, and the health official who talked to him of the desirability of vaccination—in vain!

A Ford

The terrain in the vicinity of Phoenix, Arizona is flat; it reminds one of Holland. But as one travels north, the landscape begins to change; first, slightly, later more radically.

I had been driving all morning and my motor was heating up. The sun was directly overhead, and it was therefore comforting to realize that I would not have to climb the mountain that lay ahead: obviously the road would skirt it. Unfortunately, the obvious is not always correct. Within a very few minutes after I had convinced myself that Mohammed would not have to go to the mountain, Mohammed and his chariot were going up the mountain. The total ascent was over 2000 feet; the grade was 15 degrees, and curves were all too frequent. For the first few hundred yards the car puffed along. Then, it started to boil. The road was wide enough for two cars with breathing space between. My old Buick had come to a halt at a point where it was hidden to traffic from the opposite direction; a sharp curve lay directly ahead. One usually permits a boiling car to cool, a process which can be hastened by opening the water cap. Based on past experience, I avoided the risk of scalding myself, but I succeeded in emptying the radiator of most of its water. I then tried to start the car but it would not budge. It was impossible to turn it around for the road was much too narrow; the curves prohibited a descent in reverse, and even the policy of doing nothing had its serious drawbacks, for the blocked road made a perfect setting for a collision.

Then I remembered that for the past many miles I had not passed a garage with a wrecker. Aid was far distant.

I was dolefully reflecting upon this unhappy set of circumstances when a Ford truck pulled up. I was no end surprised to see it stop, but my amazement was further increased when the driver jumped down and inquired as to my trouble. I explained that my old car just could not proceed, I dare not go back, and it should not remain where it was. The words were hardly out of my mouth when an auto swung out from behind the truck and just got back into line as a large bus came tearing around the curve. The good Samaritan was now goaded to action. He volunteered to push me up the mountain. His suggestion brought a weak smile to my face; it was clearly preposterous to expect his old Ford truck with its heavy load to push a two-ton Buick. But any alteration of the status quo could only be a change for the better. So, it seemed at the moment. But we had hardly gotten started when the first curve appeared. His front bumper lost contact with my rear one, at least it slipped, and for the next few seconds I was convinced that my Buick would soon be resting at the bottom of the mountain. There was nothing between us, except several hundred feet of air, and a little piece of bumper. But the contact held and the first curve was conquered. The difficulties however had just begun. It was not long before my savior was almost in as wretched a condition as I was; his car was heating up at a rapid rate, so rapid that it lost almost all of its power. We were moving no faster than two miles an hour. At this point the driver left his controls and told the young woman who was accompanying him—a common practice in the West for drivers would otherwise get lonely—to watch the steering wheel. He managed to loosen the hood while the truck continued at its snail's pace. Repetition made the slipping of bumpers somewhat less terrifying; but the increasing drop to the valley floor cancelled this improvement. As we approached the top, I stopped watching the outer rim; suddenly the truck driver shouted that my rear wheel had almost gone over the edge. His girlfriend however, had not lost her head and we managed to complete the curve.

Finally, a gasoline station came into view: we had arrived. Some water was put into the Ford, its driver drank a Coca-Cola and gratefully pocketed an insignificant competence. Off they were. My Buick however had to rest. It had been under a great strain.

Nogales

When trouble comes, it frequently knows no measure. Now such was the story of Nogales. Within a few years, the American garrison left, silver tumbled, high tariffs were placed upon agricultural imports and worst of all, the impossible occurred—Prohibition was repealed.

Nogales, Arizona is separated from Nogales, Mexico by a large and twisting wire fence. Some 5000 inhabitants live to the north and some 15,000 to the south. We arrived at noon and hence were in search of an eating place. There are people who love the strange and the foreign, but only from a distance; they are too frightened of the unknown to strike up an acquaintance. Now, we belonged to that group and therefore aimed to locate a restaurant on the American side of the border. An employee at the service station proved helpful. He told us that there was only one nice, clean place that served respectable food—the Continental Cafe. The information was correct: the tablecloths and napkins were white; the food was good and well-prepared. It was however, just a little startling to eat typical Eastern European dishes on the Mexican border. But Mr. Levy, the proprietor had probably discovered that the inhabitants of southern Arizona were cosmopolitan; his cafe was crowded.

At Nogales the entry into Mexico is almost completely free of red tape.

Tourists are not attracted for the city is far distant from the main route. And if they do come, they soon realize that they will have to amuse themselves, for the town offers very little. The purchase of odds and ends suggested itself as a worthy and possibly an amusing activity and we decided to make it the center of our afternoon excursion. In order to avoid future unpleasantries with U.S. Customs, we inquired, before crossing the border, of our rights and privileges. The customs officials were surprised and asked what we planned to purchase. I mentioned silver trinkets, small tapestries, shawls—in fact any trifles which would make interesting gifts. He assured us that Uncle Sam would not interfere if each of us did not bring back more than $100 worth of goods.

Then the search was on. The American town was not impressive; important chain stores had been forced to close their branches, and there were almost as many vacancies as tenants on Main Street. But Nogales, Mexico was considerably more depressing. It looked like an old harlot whose finery was torn and moth eaten. Liquor shops ad infinitum; plenty of bottles but no customers. And the price tags were not enticing. But we were more interested in silver and tapestries than in wines and whiskeys, and were therefore pleased when we reached the end of liquor row, and found ourselves at the beginning of the town's principal thoroughfare. Here were shops and people aplenty. Our expectations rose, but they quickly fell. The tinsmith, the tobacconist, and the shoemaker, were confined to small cubby-holes but their quarters seemed ample for their needs. The majority of the population lived upon the two steep slopes and spent their days tending infertile truck gardens. The salaries of the civil servants alone supplied the community with cash. The police force was equal to that of any large American city; in fact one had reason to believe from those who walked the streets or lounged in front of the city jail, that there was a police officer for every citizen.

Our search for trinkets was progressing poorly. Obviously, the town had never catered to the curiosity of bargain hunters. We walked from one end of Main Street to the other, but without success. Towards the end of our return promenade we entered a shop that had previously escaped our attention. Although the temperature outside could not have been under 100 degrees, the store was heated by a large stove. The sales clerk understood sufficient of our Mexicanized English to show us her wares, among which was some pretty silver work. Her asking price was modest, but we assumed that bargaining was in order and were therefore offered 60 percent of the price asked. She disdained to answer. We increase our offer by 10 percent; she smiled. We went up another 10 percent and she began to replace her trays. At that moment we reeled: the fire was taking command of the situation. We accepted her price, snatched our merchandise, and beat a hasty retreat.

Within a few minutes we were on the custom's line; our friend the inspector smiled and we could now appreciate the joke. Clearly, there was not a $100 worth of goods in the entire city. He asked us to show him what we had bought. Once again, he smiled, this time more broadly. He called our attention to a bit of lettering on a silver bracelet: *Made in Italy*.

A few moments later a ragged-looking farmer whose sense of equilibrium was more upset than ours, but not by the heat, attempted to reenter the States. He was caught in the act of smuggling four rotten oranges and half bottle of cactus liquor. International trade 1934!

THE MISSION

A Catholic Church and a Catholic school completely dominate the last remaining Indian reservation in the Northeast. The Yankees have helped to speed the death of the native culture. Many thousands of miles away, in the Southwest of the United States, a remnant of an Indian tribe is held together by the good offices of the Bishop of Rome. The people live in miserable huts and eke out their meager living by tilling infertile land. But their social and religious life is not as barren as their economic; the Mission is of great help to them.

Franciscan Friars have been in these parts of Arizona for many, many years. The Church of St. Xavier was built in the eighteenth century, by Spanish architects who performed the unusual task of ignoring completely the artistic traditions of their workforce. The church when completed, showed almost no signs of compromise with local art and its purity was doubtlessly highly valued by the ecclesiastical authorities.

In former years, there lived not very many miles away, a large Indian tribe that had never heard of Jesus or of Rome. They loved war and they waged war. One night, the painted warriors swooped down upon their peaceful neighbors and after killing several men and kidnapping several women, retreated to their own domain.

A few days thereafter, an old woman found in a swamp by the riverside a miniature statue of the Savior, a favorite ornament of the Mission. The attackers had taken it along, and had either lost or thrown it away. The legs had been broken off, but the pious woman brought the relic back to the church.

The friar who acts as guide, always points to the silk coverlet which is drawn up to the neck of the reclining Jesus, and points out that the natives believe the statue to be ill. He adds that the Indians are a most naive folk.

THE WHITE MAN AND THE INDIAN

The young lady was most obliging; she did her utmost to sing the praises of each and every attraction. Of course, that was her job and she performed it well. We were talking of the number of days I should spend at the Grand Canyon, and she assured me that three were the absolute minimum: a day for the descent to the river on muleback, a day of enforced rest, and a day for the points of interest along the rim.

Now the young lady knew, though she had never been to the Canyon, that a visit to the Indian House was very much worth while. It had been dedicated only a few years ago under the most unusual circumstances. Airplanes brought the chieftains from the neighboring tribes; they were to furnish the necessary local color. The summer had been very dry and the crops were in critical condition. The Indian chiefs performed a rain dance at the dedication ceremonies. That night, rain fell for the first time in many weeks.

"Funny, you never can tell what those old fellows are capable of doing."

It was just before closing time when the Indian guide pulled up a chair at the counter of the lunch room in the White Angel Camp at the Grand Canyon. He ordered an egg sandwich to be taken out. After ten minutes the waitress returned with a bag in which the sandwich was reposing. She handed it to the Indian and asked for twenty cents. Our Indian friend slowly and deliberately poured some silver from the recesses of his pocket into the palm of his hand and remarked how very inexpensive the four sandwiches really were. The girl looked at him in amazement, and then told him that he had ordered one sandwich, not four. Oh, no, the Indian was certain that he had ordered four sandwiches. The waitress became increasingly annoyed and reaffirmed with greater vehemence that the order had one been for one. The Indian again said four, and this time the girl shouted—one. At that moment a smile started to break at the corners of the Indian's mouth.

"Funny, you can never tell what those old fellows are capable of doing."

EDEN FOR SINUS

If the administration were anxious to study the problem of the decentralization of population it could find a better laboratory than the state of Arizona. Only two cities have a population in excess of 10,000—Tucson and Phoenix and neither is very large. Cacti are more common than men.

Not only economists but criminologists can study Arizona to advantage. It was in Tucson that the doughty John Dillinger was caught. There had been a fire in one of the town's three hotels and all the guests were forced to vacate their rooms. Several gentlemen harangued the firemen to move their trunks as quickly as possible. The firemen obliged and were liberally tipped for their work. Tucson reads the same magazines as do all other cities large and small. One observant fireman recognized the picture of one of his recent benefactors, and the printing beneath disturbed him. It referred to the Dillinger gang. Within four days Mr. John Dillinger was in the Pima County Jail.

The town was agog. Even patients in the last stages of tuberculosis were viewed with suspicion if they strolled within a mile of the jail. The atmosphere was not unlike that of a city in time of war: the enemy planes had been recognized and one prayed for the first bomb so that the impossible tension would finally be broken. No one in Tucson had the least doubt that Dillinger would be rescued by members of his gang, and that during the proceedings a few innocent bystanders were certain to be shot. But the populace gave no indication of their fear for during the several days that Dillinger was in jail, thousands filed past his cell. People drove from far distant places to view this most infamous and most feared citizen. Neither the Columbia football team which had upset the town during the preceding month, nor the presence of the secretary of the treasury, who had failed to upset the town were competition for Dillinger.

On the morning when the town was relieved of its distinguished prisoner, planes roared overhead, and a sleepy drunk inquired whether the United Sates had declared war on Mexico. That evening a sleepy but sober man walked along Main Street and stopped for a moment to stare in the window of a novelty shop. He had seen the Indian bracelets before and therefore passed on. Several stores beyond he stopped again, this time in front of a jewelry store. The display wares had been locked in the safe, but the center of the window was dressed. Upon closer inspection, our sleepy gentleman thought he saw a pair of silver bracelets. But why a pair? And then his eye caught the following note: "Worn by John Dillinger, Jan 22–Jan 26 while in the Pima Jail, Tucson, Arizona." And in the corner of the window were Church relics from a neighboring mission.

5

Hollywood

HERE WE ARE

Nothing is left to the imagination. The state of California does not take any chances that the tourist will fail to notice the significant difference between East and West. One can travel through forty-seven states in the union without having one's baggage inspected; but it is impossible to drive into the forty-eighth state without undergoing a rigid examination. California cannot afford to take chances; obviously, its peaches and pears must be protected. The inspector inquires whether there are any fruits or vegetables in the car, and after assurances are given that the driver hates both fruit and vegetables, a most careful search is undertaken. Pyjamas are separated. The state official is probably a churchgoer and therefore suspects a liaison between apples and pyjamas; only last week his minister delivered a sermon on original sin.

The visitor is forced to undergo a severe examination. His past is investigated in detail and his more recent activities are also surveyed. Nor is his financial position or personal life beyond scrutiny. A large car with a driver and no passengers is immediately suspect. The officials explore where the one or more passengers were left off. A few bloodstains could lead to a murder charge.

But all things come to an end. When once the inspectors have satisfied themselves that the prospective tourist is neither a communist who is attempting to smuggle in diseased fruit, nor a member of the Dillinger gang in search of hangout, they will permit him to enter. But not before they have smothered him with literature which describes the beauties of the Golden West, advertisements which sing the praises of vacationland!

Paradise

The *Drang nach Westen* has been irresistible. From every nook and corner in the country, from every stratum in society individuals and families have migrated to the Pacific coast. Some of the migrants had wealth; many more had nothing. During the past decades, Los Angeles has grown at an astonishing rate. Formerly, its chief claim to fame lay in the fact that it was but 500 miles from San Francisco; today, it is the fifth largest city in the country, a capital of a distinctive empire consisting of oil, fruits, and movies. Now the screen has become the most important of the three, not only because of the scale of its production, but even more because of its advertising. Night after night, week in and week out the people in this country and abroad are reminded of the fact that Hollywood is the Eden of America.

During the twenties, an ever-increasing stream of tourists and settlers arrived. They came to enjoy the heavenly gold, but they remained to enjoy the earthly gold. Industry boomed, real estate went on a rampage, and everybody was happy. And the upward progress continued even after the collapse of the stock market and the decline of general business in the East. Southern California was God's country and hence was exempt from the punishments meted out in the rest of the land. And so it seemed until 1931, when the special favoritism came to an end. Los Angeles slipped and slipped badly. But the city still had certain advantages. It was an ideal place to loaf just as it had been an ideal place to work: food was cheap, heavy clothing unnecessary, and fuel a minor item.

The publicity bureaus did their utmost to impress upon the stay-at-homes the beauty and attractiveness of Los Angeles. However, there were certain facts they did not broadcast. In the first place they failed to point out that the starting time of the most stupendous show of all, could never be relied upon: one never knew when the next earthquake would start.

One quiet Friday afternoon two years ago, things began to happen: cans came tumbling off the grocery shelves; tires gave the impression of having gone flat; windowpanes crashed. And many buildings cracked or tumbled. Fortunately, schools were no longer in session, for they were the major victims. Later investigation disclosed that many contractors had made the mistake of attempting to build concrete schools without concrete. This oversight would doubtless have caused the death of thousands of children had not the quake been so obliging as to postpone its appearance until 6 p.m. Throughout the night, tremors continued. People slept in their kimonos and dressing gowns so as to lose no time in making a quick exit. In many sections of the city, the inhabitants ran out into the street three or four times during the course of that night.

Several months later, a fire broke out on the outskirts of the city; park employees were clearing away some rubbish. When the flames were finally subdued, many charred bodies were found. Moreover, the sparse woodlands that surround the city had been transformed into stumps and ashes.

On New Year's Eve of that same year, the first since the repeal of Prohibition, the natives made ample preparations to celebrate in style. But the heavens decided to interfere. Rain descended as it had never descended before. Many an enterprising lad made a pretty penny that night, for instead of paying for the privilege of dancing, he was handsomely rewarded for carrying young girls in his arms. Only an angler would have dared to cross a boulevard; the gushing streams stalled automobiles wherever they appeared.

It had rained all day, and it continued to rain all night, and even during the following morning the waters from above did not cease. Many houses on the hillside were surrounded by tons of dirt; several had entirely disappeared from view; untold number of cars were partially or completely buried in the mud. Two hundred or more people departed in peace.

On New Year's Day, the Columbia and Stanford football teams met in the Hollywood Bowl. The radio announcers pointed out that the field was rather wet. The local newspapers referred to a freak storm. But the deluge was soft-peddled with the result that the rescue work was greatly hampered.

The city proper was not greatly damaged, and that is indeed unusual, for Los Angeles probably has one of the worst drainage systems in America. Many years ago the city fathers decided that it would be foolish to waste money. After all, it seldom rained; an occasional sewer would be sufficient.

Iowa on the Pacific

When the geography of this country is taught correctly, instructors will point out that there are two states by the name of Iowa: one in the Middle West, the other on the West Coast. True, the number of settlers in

"Iowa on the Pacific" is not all that large, but their purity is beyond dispute. The main square in Long Beach, their capitol, it divided into plots for horseshoe pitching and croquet. Men who once sweated in the blazing sun while harvesting their crops, now enjoy the mild climate of the coast while they pitch ringers or maneuver through wickets.

Ever since the earthquake, the population of Long Beach has declined. Conservative citizens refuse to tempt faith a second time. It is a miracle that at the time of the last quake not one of the countless oil wells that surround the city caught fire. Had but a single one ignited, southern California might have been wiped off the face of the earth.

But the migrants from Iowa and Illinois—and it is possible that the citizens from the latter state outnumber the former—were in a bad way for some time prior to the earthquake. The majority had come to the West with insufficient or just barely sufficient capital to enjoy their retirement. From the start, many found it necessary to supplement their income from savings. They opened small shops or acquired an interest in an existing business. During the last years, these investments as well as their earnings on their prior savings have fared badly. Today many an aged couple is in poor straits. Of course, they live economically for they realize that every bit of food they purchase decreases their capital. Long Beach is perhaps the most competitive market in the United States. It is not unusual for a man to walk into a drugstore, see a box of inexpensive candies, inquire of its price, and when informed that it sells for twenty-nine cents, leave empty-handed.

The majority of the people who moved from Long Beach relocated in Los Angeles. They hoped thereby to increase their physical and their economic security. Now, Los Angeles is a very large market, but not a very desirable one: competition is intense. And the city has been forced to care for a great number of unemployed, not only its own, but also the new arrivals who number as many as five hundred in a single day.

Mr. Upton Sinclair has been defeated in his race for the governorship, but the voters who supported him remain to vote another day.

WISDOM IN PARADISE

Los Angeles has many institutions of higher learning replete with distinguished faculty. Professors of hairdressing, and deans of toe manicuring can be found on every second street corner. Healers and priestesses and prophets are also present in large numbers. In fact, specialists in the soul have contributed greatly to preventing the real estate depression from degenerating into a panic. They belong to that small and exclusive group that can still afford to hire halls and hotels, for their clientele has not decreased, at least not appreciably.

The suburb of Pasadena, however, does house a true group of savants famous not only in the United States but throughout the world. These scholars devote themselves to the study of the most difficult problems; they are constantly forcing the frontier of human ignorance to retreat before their onslaughts. Their work is very intense and occasionally they lose themselves in it.

The seismologist had been anxiously awaiting an earthquake for many years so that he might be able to observe it at close range, and when the earth finally began to fault, he was walking in the garden of the Institute completely oblivious to what was happening. Despite occasional drawbacks, intense concentration is very important for scientific research.

A beautiful young lady applied to the California Institute of Technology and was informed that women were not admitted. She petitioned that an exception be made in her case for she was unable to pursue her specific researches at any other school in the vicinity and circumstances prevented her from relocating. Her preparation was investigated and the professors were satisfied that she was fully capable. However, her request was denied with an explanation that her unusual attractiveness would prove too disturbing.

PROPHETS IN OVERALLS

The boardwalk was crowded with elderly people. Many stopped to listen to a free health lecture "on the most horrible of all human scourges—the name is never mentioned in polite society—a disease which takes a yearly toll greater than the machine guns of 1918—*constipation*." Or the lecture might deal with a subject slightly less offensive to those who were brought up in an era before *Ulysses* or *Sanctuary*. The speaker would impress upon his audience that diabetes is not only curable, but curable within a very short time. And the insulin addicts need have no fear; they can be weaned away from their drug without hardship or ill effect. And the listeners after having their fill, would get up and stroll along. Occasionally, they purchased one of the many remedies which had the power to cure every disease, known and unknown, to medical science.

But these were citizens who no longer had the strength to throw horseshoes or had the patience to listen to health talks. They loved to meet and chew the rag, and the city fathers had arranged for them to congregate on the semicircular pier. Here the group, and it seldom numbered less than fifty, discuss heaven, hell, and everything in-between.

This afternoon, things were proceeding apace. Emotions were rising, but they were still under control. One man was working to round up prospective members for the revival meeting his father planned to conduct that evening. To impress the skeptics, and many of the ex-farmers from Iowa and Kansas were to be classed as skeptics, for they entertained serious doubts about important dogmas, the assistant evangelist explained: "at the beginning of time, original sin had been committed; after the passage of several centuries, Noah appeared and he was a good man. Hence evil was counterbalanced by goodness. After the flood had cleaned things up, all forces were in neutral. It was incumbent therefore on every man to realize that he must decide between God and the devil. And no one could be more helpful in the task of guiding the ignorant and the uncertain than his reverend father and himself." One of the bystanders was so rude as to question the source of the evangelist's knowledge, who replied that his insight came not from books but from his mind.

The opposition camp was assembled, a stone's throw away. A pamphlet on *Facts and Fancies of the Religion of the North* was passing from hand to hand, and occasionally a copy was sold for fifty cents. A big burly fellow explained to all who desired to listen that he was a common laborer from the oil fields at Bakersfield, who had devoted his spare time these past years to a study of the root of all evil—religion. He had written the pamphlet to enlighten the ignorant, and its composition had been carried out under the most trying circumstances. If his wife had ever caught him at the task, there would have been neither pamphlet nor oil driller. At this point one of the prospective customers who had been turning the pages of the document stated excitedly that little would have been lost had the old lady caught on. "Why look here: an average man cannot read this for the language is much too difficult; in fact there is reason to believe that the author is none too clear about the matters with which he deals. What is the sense of discussing Cro-magnon man? Who among this group had ever heard of Cro-magnon. And then again, what is an obilisque.... O∗B∗I∗L∗I∗S∗Q∗U∗E: it's certain that not more than one in a hundred know the answer. But worst of all are these big words like *imperceptible*. My God, how can anyone make sense of such writing. Now, mind you, I'm not saying that the word is wrong, or that you aren't right: but I do say that until you write for the common man like us, there isn't any sense in your writing."

At this point, the evangelist, whose success with the smaller group had obviously not been great, walked straight into the midst of the heathens and commenced to quote scripture. "God never forsook the poor and the righteous for he promised that they would be rewarded not only in heaven but also on earth." Hence they had better come this evening to the revival so that they might learn how to be worthy of the favors of the Almighty.

An old but beautifully preserved giant snickered, then began to laugh. "Is the good, kindly Lord responsible that old men have to sleep in a box with snakes rather than in a bed with pillows and blankets. He was a kindly Gent! But look here you fool, why are you whimpering and simpering about heaven and hell: don't you know that heaven and hell is right here. Well, listen: get a member of the IWW and let him start to speak right here on this bridge and see what the police will do. And then my boy, you will have had proof of how well your God takes care of the poor and the downtrodden. Of course, if you prefer, you can come with me and share my supper which will be taken from two large garbage cans one in back of the restaurant over there, and the other from behind the bakery on Elm Street."

"Trust thee in the Lord! And don't forget to come tonight."

BLISS

The traffic never ceased. From early morn to early morn a steady line of fast-moving cars passed the corner upon which he stood. Sometimes there would be a scraping of fenders and occasionally there would be a smashing of bumpers. The traffic laws were unusual. One was permitted to pass on the inside, though in case of accident the driver was held responsible; the speed limit was thirty-five miles an hour.

Throughout the day a man directed traffic: he really did not direct traffic, but when the lights turned green he would signal go, and when red flashed, his arm was erect. He was an Indian, this voluntary policeman, a wealthy Indian who had lost his mind some years ago. His wife however took care that his fortune did not go the way of his mind.

Many of the motorists, especially the steadies, got to know him and they seldom passed without saluting, and in return they never failed to receive a kindly smile. In fact, the deranged Indian always smiled, even if one were so rude as to pay no attention to his good services.

He did not have a care in the world. He was fed, housed, clothed, and permitted to amuse himself the whole long day. He harmed no one, and occasionally was of some real service: at his corner a child could cross the boulevard with safety.

TID-BITS

At Long Beach, a large cemetery marks the approach to the oil wells.

It is almost impossible to get a good orange in Los Angeles. True, oranges can be purchased very cheaply—five and eight dozen for a quarter, but they are of poor quality. The choice fruits are sent to the East.

During the early months of 1934, a western newspaper carried the following report of the meetings of a learned academy—meetings which were devoted to a discussion and evaluation of the New Deal:

"The three speakers at the banquet were: Owen D. Young, Ogden Mills, and Eugene Black."

The *Los Angeles Times* is one of the most conservative newspapers in the United States. However, on February 27th last, it carried the following bit of news about the state administration at Sacramento.

An investigation into conditions at the State Printing Office reveals that unusual schemes were developed to increase efficiency. Industrial relations were improved by fatherly kissing between employers and employees; secretaries were frequently loaned to members of the legislature; and their specific duties were left unspecified; overnight excursions between Sacramento and San Francisco were rather frequent, especially during the nice weather.

GRETA LAND

Los Angeles is a poor movie town. Many theaters stand empty and those that continue to operate frequently do so at a loss. The public demands two features, news and shorts, and from time to time a preview must be included in the program: three hours of entertainment for twenty-five cents. Every large city is able to support at least two feature houses; Los Angeles supports only one. And even this one ostentatious establishment would be hard pressed were it not that it is a point of interest for the tourist. Its courtyard has impressions of the feet of many stars. Certain celebrities were appalled at being remembered by their feet and therefore sought to enhance their chances for immortality by breaking into prose or verse. But the majority of the stars knew enough about fetishism to avoid any unnecessary embellishments.

It is impossible to be within a hundred miles of the movie community and fail to realize that the abnormal is normal, and the normal, abnormal. Never before, has a city been so heavily populated with attractive-looking young women. Pretty faces, slender bodies are the order of the day. Yet street walkers have thrived throughout the years, for many men go whoring in order to be relieved of the monotony of beauty.

Calvinistic inhibitions are thrown to the wind, and one succumbs with joy and gladness to the sensuality of the sun. From early morn until dinner time, informal dress suffices. In the leading hotels, women, young and old, can be found in shorts. Neighborhood shopping is frequently done in beach pyjamas. Men seldom wear ties, and dirty slacks are especially admired.

A million souls without roots, without values. A native is one who has lived in the city for two years, during which period he has probably changed his residence no less than four times. Poverty is scorned, for it is the denial of the good life. Money is the measure of all things, for it is the lowest common denominator.

The craving for social approval is great, insatiable. But the waitresses, chambermaids, school teachers, farm girls, and sales clerks who today fill the ranks of filmdom—they and their male counterparts—are not so fortunate as the folks back home. A society without stability, a society without culture, can have no aristocracy. Status is measured by the ownership of a sumptuous estate, custom-built cars, and exotic clothes. The tinsel and the spangle of the movies have set the tone. The aristocracy glitters.

The lack of order in the industry is without parallel and it permeates throughout. For instance, some time ago, a well-known writer contributed a short story to one of the leading monthlies, which was purchased by a major movie company for $40,000—a high price, but the author had a distinguished reputation and others were bidding. The scenario department, after attempting to adapt it, rendered the verdict—*unusable*. The author was then consulted; he promised to revise it for a further consideration of $10,000. After he had completed his job, it was again submitted to the scenarists. Once again, they turned it down. The script was then put into a cabinet and forgotten. Several months later, one of the executives ran across the story and insisted that something be done about it. A new group was assigned and after several weeks work, a scenario finally emerged. $115,000 had already been spent; but the director and the cast were yet to be selected.

But then the rush began. The picture would require three weeks of shooting. From early morning until late at night, the director, the cast, and even the stars were driven at a neck-breaking pace. Speed was of the utmost importance, for costs, once the shooting began, mount by leaps and bounds. And then it was all over. For weeks, perhaps for months, there would be nothing for anybody, star or stagehand, to do but kill time.

The reformers who are so greatly worried about the problem of leisure in a surplus economy had better study Hollywood where the problem is much more acute that in New York and Chicago. The rich, when idle, not the idle rich, are unable to amuse themselves, or at least find the task difficult. The uneducated cannot develop scientific, artistic, or literary interests. Variations in dissipations are really limited, though sex is of course the great standby. It pervades the whole of life.

Several months ago, a small group was invited to a preview of pictures in the third dimension; a young inventor was attempting to secure capital to continue his research. Selections were already being shown, when in walked one of the nation's leading stars. She had not been in the room for more than a few minutes when she interrupted the proceedings to inquire whether there were any reels with a sexy subject. The inventor apologized: no, he had none. But the actress pressed him; she simply could not be bored with scenes of machines and skyscrapers. The young man did not wish to spoil his chances of securing a patroness of great fame and wealth; he therefore told her that he had once filmed a Ceasarean operation. "Good." No, not so good; the film was at the hotel. Well, then there was nothing to do but fetch it. After an interruption of more than half an hour, the hospital scenes were flashed on the screen. They were truly remarkable, but the actress was annoyed—a Ceasarean operation is not sexy. She left in disgust.

Research in Hollywood

It is easier to assassinate a European monarch than to obtain an appointment with one of the important men in the movie industry. My introduction was of the best, a letter from an intimate friend, but that fact in no way reduced the difficulties. After three weeks of making and breaking appointments, the director's (George Cukor) secretary finally arranged for a definite meeting, though she did protect herself by stating that artists were always very unreliable.

The studios are guarded more closely than Sing Sing or the White House. However, the precautions are really unnecessary for only an explorer could ever find his way about. I must have walked a mile or more before realizing that my efforts were going nowhere. I could not locate the building in which I had my appointment, and whomever I accosted was equally ignorant. Finally a policeman crossed my path and after examining my permit and finding it in good order led me to my destination. If I had lost the scrap of paper, all would have been lost.

The secretary, despite her platinum hair, which made her look more mannequin than real, was efficient. During the hour that I awaited Cukor's arrival, she was busily engaged in aiding the tax attorney to rescue her employer from the 30 percent bracket. No slip of paper had been mislaid; no bill had been destroyed. Nor had delicate feelings stood in the way of recording bad debts from good friends. The movies might cater to the romantic tastes of the populace, but the work force knew the difference between illusion and reality. The tax attorney was so well versed in the bypaths of the law that he completed his assignment within the hour. If Washington should ever decide to check his work, it would have to assign a staff of lawyers whose investigations would probably keep them busy for a month.

When Cukor finally arrived more than an hour late, the entire office became upset, they had not really expected him to arrive. He was pleasant and apologetic: pleasant because he was happy to see a friend of his good friend, apologetic because he had been negligent in not having arranged an earlier appointment. We began to chat.

"In the movies, especially among directors, success depends upon native talent: education is more or less meaningless. Take Mr. R. The census administrators would classify him as a moron, he never speaks, he only mumbles. He derives stimulation from the vilest perfumes and the cheapest jazz music. And yet, this is the point, he has more talent, and produces finer pictures, than any man in the industry.

"Let's look at my case. I know nothing about economics; I can't understand the beginning of all this discussion about inflation and the gold standard. Russia is a closed book to me, though I must admit that I sympathize heartily with any plan which increases the economic welfare of the masses. In fact, I know nothing about costs, scenarios, and the like. But give me a script and if I say that it can be used, let me go ahead. The company will not lose any money on my guess. If the executives, however, were so foolish to ask me to outline my plans in detail, they would receive no answer, and I would direct no picture. In the movies, it's solely a question of trusting the individual; either he can or he cannot deliver the goods—but there is surely no way of figuring it out ahead of time by looking at budgets. But research and analysis does have its place in the scheme of things. I am just laying the groundwork for the production of an English classic. I am leaving for England within the next few days in order to become better acquainted with the scene, and also to find actors for character parts. If you would be interested, we might run over to research division and see what they have today."

A brisk walk through the courtyard and we arrived in front of a low and comely building. Obviously, it was not used for technical purposes and at the same time, its simplicity led one to doubt that it housed either directors or stars. The bungalow stood apart; it was different. Upon crossing the threshold, one was even more surprised. The interior decorations were in good taste, and the lady in charge was clearly a lady. Etchings, books, and small pieces of art were arranged throughout the rooms by one who had never been impressed by Mr. DeMille's gigantic productions. But the most unusual sight was the quantity and quality of the books both on the reference shelves and on the desks of the several assistants.

The librarian was in excellent spirits for she had just received a large shipment of books from England which she knew would be of the greatest value to the director in preparing his next picture. We were ushered into her private office, where we found the desk and chairs stacked high with books. Cukor made straight for them; his eagerness matched that of a confirmed bibliophile. One after another, the importations were taken up, fingered, and replaced. The process was accomplished with lightening speed: thirty seconds or a minute were devoted to each book. Cukor became annoyed: the new arrivals did not please him. Suddenly, he exclaimed: "My God, did you ever hear of people writing books without pictures?"

BEHIND THE SCREEN

The average movie which just fails to bore the average moviegoer costs about $250,000 to produce. Many of the large companies have a high overhead, amounting to 30–40 percent; hence, a $250,000 picture is frequently completed with a cash outlay of only $150,000.

The day of the superproduction is said to be nearing its end. The companies no longer have the money to finance themselves to the tune of a $1,000,000 for one picture, and the banks are frightened to extend that much credit for a single production. There are perhaps no more than three firms in the industry that can be reasonably certain not to lose money on expensive pictures.

A recent success showed the following cost breakdown:

The star's salary	$100,000
Supporting cast	100,000
Technical staff	30,000
Stage, costumes, etc.	150,000
Film, retakes	20,000
Rent	30,000
Incidentals	20,000
Overhead	50,000
Total	$500,000

During the boom days, the industry never had to think twice about money. The large receipts from the theaters, and the sale of new stock, flooded Hollywood with dollars. It is only in recent times that the movie companies have been forced to deal with the banks. And they have found their new taskmasters difficult. Several bankers aimed to take over their customers' company but before long, they found that this was not a winning way.

The financing of pictures, rather than the financing of film companies, is the safest way to go. One banker with twenty years experience reported that he had lost only one small loan. There are difficulties in extending credit to movie makers, but the expert is not dismayed. Cost sheets are difficult to interpret; loans are usually unsecured and run for a considerable period of time; warehouse receipts are meaningless. Success or failure depends on the banker's knowledge of the movie industry and the movie people. Most bankers know neither the industry nor the people.

A Palace Royal

San Marino, California is one of the most remarkable towns in the entire country, that is if one is willing to identify a community by its most important institution. When the oil fields have run dry, and when the movies have been forgotten, a few visitors will still find their way to southern California if only to visit the Huntington Estate.

Mr. Huntington's collection of English paintings are rivaled only by the masterpieces that hang in the National Gallery in London. But the Gainsboroughs, Reynoldses, Romneys and Lawrences which decorate the walls in the Huntington home, are in a well-nigh superb setting. The furniture, the carpets and the draperies, not to mention the light, the air and the view, all conspire to make the museum unique.

Incredibly the library is almost of equal distinction. In fact, there is reason to believe that Mr. Huntington was even more interested in books than in paintings. He brought manuscripts and books by the crate, and as the cataloging proceeds the rarest and the most valuable items become available for others to study and enjoy. The exhibition cases are frequently changed, but it is possible to view at one time: the Gutenberg Bible, the Receuills de Troyes—the first book printed in England, a first edition of Dante, First Folio of Shakespeare, and the first edition of the King James Bible.

The collections are open to the public, but Mr. Huntington was interested that they not only be admired but used. He therefore established reading fellowships in order to facilitate research. A scholar is now able to come and spend six months or a year at the Library at San Marino. Free from material worries, he can devote his entire day to the volumes which cry out for attention. But there are several students who are attracted more by the sumptuous gardens without, than by the hard tables within. And no one interferes.

6

People and Places

THE FAMILY

Evening was approaching and dinner was not far distant. We had completed our conference. "Would I come home and break bread with them?" "Why yes, I should be very happy to do so if I could rearrange my other appointments." A few telephone calls and all was in order.

My host had proved during the course of the afternoon to be well informed not only about his own industry but about the world of business. His knowledge was considerable without being overwhelming; his judgments were acute without being brilliant. In short he was a solid man of affairs.

The journey home took a considerable time. One can travel long distances to and from work in cities other than New York. The car slowed down as we passed through a typical upper middle-class neighborhood where the homes were undistinguished but substantial. We finally stopped in the midst of Babbitt Land.

The house was furnished in good taste, nothing too old, nothing too modern. A harmony of 1933. My hostess seemed not in the least perturbed by the short warning her husband had given her that he was bringing a guest home for dinner.

We were six at dinner: husband, wife, the husband's mother, two children—a boy of ten and a girl of thirteen, and myself. The day had been cold and our appetites were in good working condition; the hot food disappeared in the shortest, polite interval. Conversation was almost unnecessary, surely a luxury. But then I did have to submit to the usual run of questions: from whence I hailed, my work, my destination, my background, my likes, dislikes—in fact I was forced to run the gamut. It was not very long before the dessert made its appearance and by that time the attack upon the food had slackened: we had also managed to strain the resources of cross-examination. The customary run of questions was exhausted and it was not considered polite to continue in the same vein. Perhaps the visitor did not feel free to discuss at length some of his tastes and preferences. But it proved devilish hard to maneuver the conversation into another channel. Fortunately, the hostess had the insight to suggest a change of scene. We moved to the living room.

Now conversation was completely unnecessary. The company had divided itself into spectators and participants at a wrestling match. Father and son were engaged in headlocks, arm twists, legholds and the like: we, in the ringside seats, could admire the dexterity of the young boy as he grappled with the older man. The performance lasted some ten minutes, and only at its conclusion did anybody find it necessary to explain what had transpired. The suddenness of the onslaught had surprised no one but myself, for the tussle was routine, the usual substitute for the demitasse.

The next few minutes were taken up with the departure of the children who had lessons to do and the enforced relaxation of my host who tried desperately to get his blood pressure down. Soon, quiet reigned once again: the two women were knitting and the two men were staring. The hostess had escaped for some minutes, but on her return the tension mounted. Words just would not begin to flow. The awkwardness was mounting. I mentioned Heidelberg. The reaction was instantaneous. For minutes, perhaps for scores of minutes, I recounted stories of duels and good-looking Katis; of songfests and torchlight processions. I tried hard to color my recital with the proper Hollywood background, for the screen had been the major instrumentality in acquainting the group with oldest and most romantic of German universities. Hegel and Bunson could not hope to compete.

But a monologue with an occasional exclamation is not a substitute for social conversation. I soon became self-conscious and started to quiet down, and it was not long before I stopped talking. This time conversation did not lag. We began to discuss American universities. At the outset, a disagreement arose as to the significance of collegiate football. The man of business was certain that if a modern corporation could not sell its products without the aid of advertising it was likewise impossible for a college to progress without the publicity that accompanied victories on the gridiron. Furthermore an interest in sports could alone prevent the students from becoming too studious. Nothing could be worse than a school populated by bookworms. I answered in some heat that the argument did not hold water. Did any corporation ever advertise products other than their own? No. Well, why should institutions of higher learning advertise football rather than learning? "An uneducated public"— but how could a successful football team prove to a merchant in Tuscon that Harvard's victory over Ohio State really proved it to be a superior institution. And what if Ohio State won? Was it not indiscreet to pressure large universities that were concerned with matters academic to spend time, money, and energy in developing a football team to justify their departments of philology and pathology. Can one not argue by analogy from the world of business that many successful corporations started on the road to ruin by leaving the sheltered environment of their specialty market.

The hostess now entered the argument on my side, more out of conviction than politeness. (She had once taught school and remembered the struggles between arithmetic and baseball). But it was not long before the argument came to and end for the participants had developed their respective positions in full and had no more to add.

There were great difficulties in finding a new subject to discuss for all of us wanted to avoid another heated controversy. Fortunately, there are always a few safe subjects such as the weather, the most recent movies, the approaching holiday season. But the islands of safety were few and they were soon exhausted. The clock struck and all of us were reminded that it was only 8:30 and we could therefore expect no relief for at least another two hours. Bridge was mentioned but the older lady remarked that her playing was so poor that she preferred to continue with her knitting. Finally my host as if inspired, asked whether I would enjoy ping-pong. I responded enthusiastically and we excused ourselves and proceeded to the basement where the table was located.

Outside the thermometer was hovering around ten, but it was not long before we were in shirt-sleeves. We both played seriously; we played to win. We were evenly matched, and the score zigzagged back and forth. My host let out an Indian yell at each successful recovery of a difficult ball; his enthusiasm in winning was matched only by his depression in losing. The score stood three to three and we arranged that the seventh would be the last set. Once again, the games broke evenly; finally the deciding points approached. I struck out to win but at that moment I saw the image of my defeated opponent; the next balls went wild. He had won.

We returned upstairs and I was certain that it was late enough to beat a polite retreat. But no, the hands of the clock turned slowly—it was only 9:20. The children came in to say goodnight—9:30. A few words about them, a few more about ping-pong—9:40. Then silence. This time, I was inspired; did they ever play three-handed bridge? The table was set, the cards dealt, the score recorded. The next time that I looked at my watch, the hand was on eleven. An invitation to come again if I remained in town until the end of the week. My thanks for the pleasant evening; leavetaking.

Dr. C.

Somewhere in the Middle West there is a man who has lived a very long life; he is older than the oldest of the patriarchs and as wise as the wisest of them. He has lived and relived the last five thousand years. No country in the Near East or Europe is unknown to him—Egypt, Palestine, Syria, Persia, Greece, Rome, Spain, France, England, Germany, Poland, and Russia. He was born for the ninth, the nineteenth, the ninetieth time in Russia while Alexander sat on the throne. It was the last of the Alexanders and there was only one more Nicholas between him and the end of the Romanoffs.

Dr. C. had a happy childhood. True, he belonged to a race that was proscribed from living within the confines of any large city, a race that was treated upon occasion much more poorly than the draft animals of the peasants. But there are always exceptions: the position of a few Jews who were accepted for one reason or another into Russian society was superior to that of their coreligionists in countries where Jews could become prime-ministers. Dr. C.'s family was persona grata.

Archangel was and probably still remains more remote from European or other civilizations than Siberia or Turkistan. Dr. C. found himself as a young man in one of the most northerly villages of this northern peninsula. The czar had no extra kopeks to spend upon its inhabitants and they were totally illiterate. However, one old peasant knew how to read and he managed to entertain his many relatives and friends. The Bible was his mainstay. Dr. C. became friendly with the old man and spent many hours in conversation with him. One day, Jews were mentioned. The old serf became tremendously excited for though he had been reading of these people for many years, he knew nothing about them.

"Would Dr. C. please tell him how Jews looked? Was their skin red like the devils?"

"No, not red."

"That's funny, well then, they must have cloven feet."

"No."

"Then they surely must have horns."

"No."

"Then how do they look?"

"Frankly, my good man they look just like you and me."

"But that's impossible master. You are fooling me, fooling an old, ignorant man. Really, it's not my fault that I have never had a chance to see a Jew. I am stupid but I am not so stupid to believe that a Jew looks like you and me. Why, that's impossible!"

"Well, old man, if you really want to see a Jew look at me—I'm one."

"Ha, ha, my good sir that is a fine, a very fine joke. But please stop teasing an old man."

"But I *am* a Jew."

"Oh, please don't tease an old man…"

Milady

People go to Washington because they have been elected to go there; people go to Washington because they have failed to be elected to go there; and people go to Washington. Milady was one who chose to go to Washington, at least twice a year.

They met at the Capitol one morning. Both had forgotten that the Supreme Court did not assemble until high noon, and they therefore had two hours on their hands. The guard suggested that they might be entertained by the Senate committee that was at the very moment investigating a prominent banker. The idea seemed a good one; they strolled down the hall towards the elevator.

The discussion soon centered on the New Deal. "Was the young man a good Democrat?" This was the first time that he awoke from his academic naivete and realized that his reaction to Professor Warren's gold theories of Secretary Wallace's pig massacres was to be predicated not on economic theory or statistics but on the political faith of his father and grandfather. Too bad. His grandfather had never heard of the Democratic party, his father was an enrolled Democrat, and he was interested in economic theory and statistics. But Milady was a good Democrat and yet she was no end disturbed by some of the recent tendencies. "I just can't stomach the NRA, it doesn't make any sense. Why, I could never run my household if the hours of the servants were limited. My poor husband would have to go without his dinner if he arrived too late, and the children would not be attended to if they arrived too early. Moreover, these strikers are simply horrible; here, they have these short hours and still they are not satisfied. It's hard not to lose one's faith in the Democratic party, but let's hope that the Supreme Court will help us out." (At that moment the elevator arrived and they went down and waited for the underground subway to take them to the Senate Building).

"What do you think of the Court? Rather a remarkable group of men, I should say."

"Frankly, madam, now that Mr. Holmes is no more, I find only two of the nine justices to be truly interesting—Brandeis and Cardozo."

"Oh, Mr. Justice Brandeis, why yes, my husband and he were members of the same boat club many years ago—that was when we still lived in Boston. And he attended to the legal work of both my husband and myself. Quite a remarkable man considering the fact that.... oh, you are not by any chance, a, a Jewish?"

"No, not by chance, by birth."

"A most remarkable man, a most remarkable man..."

The subway just would not come!

GOING TO THE RACES

My car stopped and in jumped two lads. They were on their way to Saratoga to see the turf fly. During the past two years they had failed to sneak away from home but the recollection of their earlier excursions still remained vivid. Today's jaunt had great significance. It presaged the return of the good old times when they had made weekly trips to the track. Only a few days ago, their father's wages had been increased from ten to fourteen dollars; true, that was still considerably below the thirty he had once earned, but still, the turn had come.

They were natives of Italian heritage but they murdered English as expertly as the Mafia had once murdered their relatives. And yet, their parents had been in this country sufficiently long to forsake the teachings of the Vicar of Rome in favor of the preachings of the Anglican minister, Mr. Malthus. However, we managed to chat and it was not very long before we were at the track. I wished them a pleasant afternoon and hoped that they would have no difficulty in finding the loose boards that were their tickets of admission. They thanked me for the ride and assured me that they would enjoy themselves heartily, despite the fact that at the Saratoga races there were always so many Negroes, Jews, and other foreigners.

PEACE ON EARTH

The ladies were dozing, the men were bored, and the speaker gave every indication that he was knew it. This was the third meeting of the Good Will Group that had been formed several months ago for the purpose of increasing harmony among the members of the three religions. Several prominent men in the community believed that the crude antagonisms and prejudices between the members of different faiths could be eradicated or at least lessened by frequent social and intellectual contacts.

The president was an ex-Yankee who had spent the greater part of his life on the West Coast: his intelligence, learning, and behavior stamped him as an unusual man. The host for the evening was the reform rabbi. The group numbered twenty-five or more: two Catholic priests, a Presbyterian, a Congregationalist and a Unitarian minister, several judges, professional and business people, more or less evenly divided between the three faiths.

Many guests had never been in the home of a rabbi and during the first few minutes after their arrival, they were slightly nervous. But they soon discovered that the walls were lined with beautiful sets of Dickens, Thackeray and Scott: there were no old and musty Hebrew tomes in view. Moreover, the furniture and the decorations were neither foreign nor esoteric; no, just the usual embellishments one would expect in the home of a successful bourgeois.

The Congregationalist minister was speaking on the unhappy state of affairs that made it necessary for the Good Will Group to be called into existence. It was a blot on Western civilization that organizations had to be formed for the purpose of helping neighbors to live in peace. But he was frank in admitting that such movements were necessary and he was happy to note that they were increasing throughout the length and breadth of the land. In answer to the question whether the missionary activities of the Protestant churches did not impede interfaith cooperation, the minister pointed out that there existed a distinct cleavage between the conservatives and the liberals. The left wing, to which he belonged, did not look with favor upon missionary activities and he was therefore loath to offer a defense of missions, but if a defense were necessary it was pertinent to note that Protestants devoted almost all of their efforts to converting the heathen, i.e., Zulus, Chinese, Hindus, and the like.

The host spoke next. He explained that the Jews could contribute very little but their prayers to the present undertaking for they did not have to be encouraged to live in peace with their neighbors. They were victims of prejudices, not creators of prejudices. True, the charge had been made from time to time that they were an exclusive and stiff-necked people, but any unbiased observer would admit that their isolation was dictated by others, not chosen by themselves. The rabbi concluded his remarks with a stirring appeal for a revision of the Sunday School curriculum that he felt was in no small measure responsible for the anti-Semitism that prevailed.

The Catholic priest was the last to take the floor and he introduced his subject by dwelling on the inherent difficulties that confronted his Church when it attempted to cooperate in interfaith movements. He knew that many present wondered why the Catholic Church alone refused to take part in a communal Thanksgiving service. The explanation was really very simple. "There exist certain absolute truths, and these cannot be compromised. Now the Church bases its religious services upon these absolute beliefs and hence it must demand of all its members that they worship according to the established ritual. Of course, the Church is perfectly willing to acknowledge the rights of nonbelievers to pray as they see fit; but the Church cannot compromise. For instance, if a chiropractor, a homeopath, a Christian Scientist, and a reputable surgeon were called in on a case, they would be likely to disagree about the diagnosis, and they would assuredly disagree about the therapy. Now, nobody would suggest that the surgeon should modify his ideas or his interventions in order to approximate more closely the opinions of the others." The priest, however, pointed out that the Church is desirous of aiding to the greatest extent of its ability all movements aimed at increasing harmony among men, for the Church itself suffered grievously from oppression in Russia, in Mexico, and in Germany.

The spark was off; Germany had been mentioned. Within a few seconds a chorus of vituperation was audible. At last, a common basis had been found: all agreed. The evening was advancing and the hostess therefore decided to pour tea. Shortly thereafter the party broke up.

On the drive into town, the president passed his country club and thought that it might be a good idea to stop and have a drink. But he suddenly remembered that the Jewish physician and the Catholic judge who were riding with him would not be welcome.

The Chosen People

H.J. did not share the general prejudices of Southerners for the Children of Israel, for he was no Southerner. On the other hand, he was not overfond of the descendants of Abraham, Isaac, and Jacob. And justly so.

For many years ago, in his native land, he underwent three most disturbing experiences. He was born and bred in one of the industrial cities of England. As a young man he had occasion to court one of the daughters of Esther, for he found her comely. Her family however, soon put an end to his advances for their daughter would not receive their permission to marry one the uncircumcised.

Soon thereafter, H.J. found himself once again face to face with the defenders of the true faith; this time he asked a favor which he thought could not be denied, not even to the unbelieving. He desired to join their golf club; it was but a stone's throw from his house while the other clubs were at the other end of town. After due deliberation, for the members were somewhat at a loss as how to proceed, his application was turned down. He was informed that the board decided that the admission of a stranger would place both the stranger and members on the defensive, an attitude that would be uncongenial to all.

At the turn of the century when H.J. was a student at the University, Palestine was a piece of arid land belonging to an indolent ruler who spent his time in Constantinople. For one reason or another, H.J. thought that his friends in the North would gain greatly if their native land would again be under their control. He set about to study population, acreage, crop yields, land prices, and the like. It was not very long before he came to the simple conclusion that most of the land could be purchased very cheaply. Now H.J. knew that if the wealthy and well-to-do Jews the world over would contribute to a joint fund, the money could be raised without great difficulties.

But once again, these queer people acted queerly. They simply were not interested. Since then, H.J. has lost interest.

HITLER MOVES WEST

The executives of the bank were in conference; in fact it was an executive meeting, but there was little to discuss. Deposits were decreasing, bond prices were falling rapidly, and the cash reserves were being rapidly depleted. One lived in constant fear of a run or ruin. Whate'er the morrow brings, it could only be sorrow.

The men looked at each other but said nothing. What was there to say? Finally the silence was broken. A young vice president began to speak. He admitted that the economic morass has set him to thinking, and about a month ago he first stumbled upon the problem of the Jew. Since then, he had pursued the subject intensely, and the result of his investigations led him to suggest that the bank cease making loans to Jews. There could be no doubt that they were untrustworthy, and extremely dangerous debtors. Clearly they care little for reputation: rather a bad name and much money, than a good name and no money. The majority of the executives had not taken to scholarly pursuits and they were neither impressed nor unimpressed by the observations of their young colleague. The president, however, had been reading and thinking ever since the depression of the 1890s and he did not remain silent. He suggested that the matter be tabled for a month; in the interim he would put two clerks to work on checking the records.

The subject was never referred to again; the president informed the young man that the files proved that no Jew had ever defaulted on his loan, not one in the last thirty years.

One day, the young man will probably be president of the bank.

RED FLASH

"Buddy, see that nice, brick house over there right in the middle of the wells; not much to look at now, but you should have seen it a few years back. Gee, not much left, not even memories...

"We were coming out of the field one Friday evening, feeling pretty happy because Saturday was a short day and then the weekend. One of the gang pointed to the horizon; seemed as if something was going on but we paid no attention to it. Next morning on the way out to work even more seemed to be happening over there; looked like a wildcatter which had struck oil. On Monday morning, after a swell weekend in town, I sure remember it, we went over to see what all the hullabaloo was about. Well, there sure was plenty of digging, moving, hauling going on, and as we stood around more and more people seemed to come from nowhere. Would you believe it that by the end of the week, there was a regular community over there. The storekeeper was selling his goods before they arrived and even old John D. wouldn't have put up his nose at the profits. And by the end of the week, the old lady had her wooden house finished, the one before she built the brick one. Hell, I've never been able to figure out how she did it so quickly: must have kidnapped the carpenters. And boy, she had the girls there; finest lot, the country round. And her liquor wasn't half bad. Of course, she charged good and plenty but who cared? They were all making money to beat the band.

"And once she caught her breath, she tore down the old wooden building, and it wasn't a bad one at that, and built this swell looking brick place; and she sure didn't save any on furnishing it.

"The furniture sure was swell. But she could afford it. The money was coming in so quick, she couldn't count it.

"Then one day, must have been six months after they opened up, rumors came through that the wells weren't doing so good; next day the reports were worse, and within no time they shut down.

"Yes sir, had some nice times in that old brick house..."

Behold the Word of God

The East is always making incorrect judgments about the rest of the country. Many assumed that evangelism died when the last state was admitted into the union. Only the enterprising activities of certain theatrical directors in New York managed to prove to the frequenters of the Great White Way that they were greatly mistaken. The retort has often been made that evangelism on a stage or in a hotel is not comparable to evangelism in the raw. Quite true. But when a minister can address, during a fifteen-week campaign, a quarter of a million people, the evidence cannot be easily controverted. Evangelism lives and thrives.

It was winter in a cold and blasty city. Meetings were held twice a day; at noon, and at eight o'clock in the evening. The theater was well heated, the seats were comfortable, and the music was agreeable. Admission was free. The assistant director of revivals held the stage for about an hour. His was a difficult task for the audience was primarily interested in the person who was to follow. But the novice did very well. His excellent speaking voice and his accomplished gestures stood him in good stead when he delivered his tirades against the clergy of the city. He accused them of cowardice and slander. Not only were they afraid to invite the visiting evangelist to share their pulpits, but they spread despicable calumnies about his character and his work. The audience was awakened out of its indifference and commenced to applaud the attacks upon the local ministers.

After the invectives had been delivered, the assistant reported on the excellent results of the previous meetings and then concluded his remarks by delivering the most lurid encomiums about the speaker of the evening.

Then the meeting began in earnest. He who had heard the call of God must have possessed hidden virtues and charms, for they were clearly not discernable to the ordinary mortal. His physique was undistinguished, his voice was undistinguished, and his ideas were undistinguished. No, perhaps the last statement is not completely true.

The argument against evolution was indeed original. "According to Mr. Darwin and his learned followers, the steps of human development are usually said to have progressed from plants to insects, from insects to birds, from birds to humans. Now even an ignorant farmhand knows—but alas how much more stupid are our professors than our farmers—that if insect life were not constantly destroyed by birds and other animals, the world would be a world consisting solely of bugs and ants. In fact there is reason to believe that the learned scholars really understand this point. How can it be explained therefore that birds appeared on the earth after insects; how could they have survived? Clearly, the learned are illiterate; their logic is false. But still these men have the effrontery to blaspheme the word of God. Their sin is not only venial but deadly. But the evil which these false teachings have caused is very great.

"One need but recall that it was the German philosopher, Frederick Neizger [sic] who popularized the theory of the superman which was based upon the fallacious doctrine of evolution. And with what result? Two rich boys in the Chicago area—Leopold and Loeb—who had read his works recently murdered a young friend in order to prove to themselves and to the world that they were truly supermen.

"What have churches done to cope with this problem? You will be interested to know that a census last Sunday evening taken in all the churches along Woodward Avenue showed a total attendance of 700; that is an answer in itself.

"Few people know that fifty cents out of every dollar eventually goes to the state for the prevention or the punishment of crime. The average criminal costs the community $2,000. Now, $1 can save a man. Your contributions tonight will therefore bring a return of 2000 percent. All you have to do is believe in the word of God."

POLITICS

Despite the reputation of Tammany Hall, New York cannot hope to compete with Chicago, where the spoils system is unusually efficient: police; voters, judges. A prominent member of the judiciary ventured the surmise that during the reign of Al Capone, there was not a single member of the police force who was not on Capone's private payroll.

The mores of the Windy City are indeed remarkable. A man will enter a court of law and present a letter to the judge. Its contents almost never vary. The local district leader begs to inform His Honor that the bearer of the note is a close friend and that any courtesies shown him will be greatly appreciated. An ambitious man cannot afford to ignore such entreaties. Only recently a young and honest judge informed an important political figure that he planned to decide cases on their merit. After the next election, the brave gentleman discovered that he would no longer be afforded the opportunity of deciding cases. However, he entertained serious doubts as to the arithmetical abilities of the poll tabulators, and therefore petitioned his former colleagues to grant a court order for a recount. But his efforts were in vain. The older men remembered what the youngster forgot, that political bosses are by definition competent statisticians. At the end of a year an out-of-town judge was sitting in Chicago; he finally acceded to the request for a recount. Only two boxes were opened before incumbent retired in favor of the contestant.

The city has corrupted the state. During the last gubernatorial election the Republican candidate held rallies every noon at a large theater. Admission was for men only. A stage show was presented that compared favorably with anything that was produced in the side streets of Marseilles. The attendees could see for themselves that the impresario was a regular fellow, and they were asked to take it on faith that he would make a good governor.

But the Republicans, fearing a Democratic landslide, could not afford to ignore the opposition's candidate. In campaigning downstate, the advisers of Mr. Thompson made every effort to snare the votes of the corn and hog farmers. The populace was reminded that the Holy Writ forbade the Children of Israel to eat ham and pork. Hence, there could be no doubt that if Judge Horner were elected, he would proscribe the raising, and prevent the selling of hogs. This analysis is said to have cost the Democratic nominee many thousand of votes.

One fights best when the struggle is uneven. Theatricals and biblical exegesis did not exhaust the bag of tricks. The Republicans rounded up in the ghetto of Chicago, a group of old Jews with long beards, long coats, and long hair and shipped them downstate with instructions to call on individual farmers and say: "Pleeze mister, wote fur mein brodder, Chudge Orna."

THE BENEFACTOR

It was in the days before Henry Ford that John Smith reigned supreme. He was a man of varied interests. Among other things, he owned the finest gambling establishments, houses of recreation, and saloons. His holdings stretched far and wide; in fact, he was the owner of several important enterprises across the border in Windsor. But when all was said and done Smith was very much a patriot and a local chauvinist. His holdings of Detroit real estate were a constant reminder of his faith in the future of his beloved city.

During his lifetime he had exerted himself to offer the best in entertainment. Now, he feared that his heirs would be less considerate and he therefore willed a large tract of land in the Detroit River to the city. A large and free public park was to be established. The bequest carried only one stipulation: a large statue of the benefactor had to be erected in a conspicuous place in the park.

For many years, the virtuous burghers were sorely perplexed, for though many admired Smith privately, nobody dared to honor him publicly. But the gift was too large to be refused. After long and careful study, a solution was finally worked out. A life-size statue of Mr. John Smith would be placed at the end of the island with the front facing the Canadian shore and with the back to the park.

The provision of the will was fulfilled; the moral scruples of the clergy were respected, but international complications were barely avoided.

THE LEARNED JUDGE

Many years ago, the railroad had transported into the Southwest a large number of Chinese coolies for road work. The native population fearing for their jobs, which they decided belonged rightfully to them, applied the most extreme pressure on the railroad to withdraw the Asiatics. The company finally acceded to their demands. Only one Chinaman remained: he was the crew cook. Orientals can prepare food much more cheaply than Westerners.

Now the Chinaman was a quiet and inoffensive person, and his meals were if not excellent, at least satisfactory. The community having forced the railroad to give way on the road gang, decided to cinch its victory by insisting on the recall of the cook. The corporation balked: they would not remove him. The hotheads then suggested to Loo Sing that he had better leave for the climate in these parts never agreed with Asiatics, and, in fact, they could guarantee that it would fail to agree with him. Loo Sing acted dumb.

Two weeks later his body was found suspended from a tree. the sheriff had no difficulty in identifying the lynchers for they bragged of their handiwork. But they were never brought to trial. The local judge refused to issue warrants for their arrest for he had failed to discover a statute that prohibited the hanging of Chinamen.

THE INDUSTRIOUS RICH

He was a philosopher and a student of philosophy, but he had no need to strain his eyes by candlelight or contend with oil and wicks. His father had possessed the foresight to accumulate sizable means so that his son might spend his days in study.

Upon graduating from college some ten years ago, he did not set out for Paris, as so many young men do, to study art and to study life. No, his American professors had impressed him sufficiently; they had kindled in him a love for the truth—for the spirit rather than for the flesh.

But then, the tradition of the flesh was also very strong. The young man felt that it would not be proper for him to live entirely upon the bounty of his father. He therefore devoted his mornings to business so that in the years to come his sons in turn might have the same opportunities as his father had provided him. But from noon unto night, the young man's devotion to learning was pure and unadulterated. No, not quite. The first hour or two of the afternoon was spent in earthy pursuits.

I had the pleasure of meeting him at one of these preparatory sessions, and to the best of my recollection the exercises were quite strenuous—exotic fruits, heavy soups, red roasts—but it is all hazy for my attention was otherwise directed.

Our philosopher had entered upon a Socratic dialogue. He asked whether I believed that the machine was here to stay? I ventured to guess that for the next century of two the machine would not disappear unless we disappeared—which of course was not impossible now that we had created such efficient engines of destruction. He then informed me that I had missed the purport of his interrogation. Philosophers never talk about such short time periods as centuries; "here to stay" referred to millennia. After all, the Middle Ages are really a very small segment of European history.

"Philosophers must deal with long stretches of time for else their work would be of little value. They seek the truth so that they can teach the truth; and if they are successful, future generations will live a happier and fuller life. But the discovery of categories is a slow and laborious process, and few students would be willing to devote themselves to this work if they did not for know that they could influence the course of mankind not fifty or a hundred but five hundred and a thousand years hence." The category of the roast beef!

Gentlemen All

I came to get my car, which had been left for greasing, and in paying my bill, I asked whether all the parts had been carefully checked for tomorrow's trip would take me into wild country. The attendant inquired where I planned to drive and upon mentioning my route, he assured me that he was well acquainted with the roads and if I had the time, he would be most happy to give me a pointer or two. And that is how it all started.

Dusk was approaching and business was light. Our conversation got off to a good start; conversation is really not the correct word, for I hardly opened my mouth. Roger Nagol talked.

"My grandfather, who was a general in the War between the States, was born near Selma where the family had lived for a hundred years. His father and grandfather were wealthy people, and at the outbreak of the war the family owned 3,000 acres and 400 slaves; their net worth could not have been less than $250,000. At the close of the war, my grandfather has his acres and seventeen cents in his pocket, and within a short time, he had only the seventeen cents. Exorbitant taxes were levied upon people who did not possess enough capital to work the land, and soon the estates fell under the auctioneers' gavel. And then the carpetbaggers. They finished what Sherman began, and between the two, the job was well done!

"Today, the culture of yesterday, is no more. The old aristocrats are gone. Well, a few families have survived but they are almost without exception impoverished. Of course, there are many wealthy individuals in the South and several of them have not only made but inherited money. But everyone knows that they are not the true bluebloods.

My grandfather died poor, very poor but my father managed to resurrect the family fortune, at least to some small degree. But then, in the fall of 1929 the tricky Northerners—I hope you will forgive my saying so—took his money away. That's why you see me here, working for a few dollars a week for Mr. Rockefeller and his associates. But I don't complain though it is awful hard to forget that my family were millionaires when old John D. didn't have enough to eat. Sometimes, I fear that we are a dying race, we old Southerners: I can hardly lift the sword which my grandfather was able to swing with grace. He was six foot four and more, and look at me—a bare five-five.

"But it is a great shame that after the war the North didn't give the South back to the Southerners; there is a slight chance that we might have made something of it. Surely we could not have made a worse mess than now exists. Sure, we exploited the Negroes for many years but we learnt something from the war. Young men from the North sacrificed life and limb to free the slaves. Now, that left an impression on us. We were willing to readjust but, my God, the change couldn't come overnight. We could not transfer a culture which had taken us two thousand years to build, in a few months to a people who had spent their lives picking cotton and fishing. The North gave the Negro nothing—when it promised him forty acres and a mule. But it could have given him so much, if it only knew, or if it had only asked. Education was the crying need and yet nothing was done about it, and even today progress has been very slow.

"Look at my helper, George, over there. Why, it's almost impossible to find a more beautiful specimen of mankind: and his intellectual abilities are on a par with his physical qualities. Somehow or other, he learned to read and write, and there is little doubt that his mind is better than mine or most of my friends. But look at the bad deal which he has received. He works for Mr. Rockefeller for a few cents a day, greasing cars and filling gas tanks, instead of which he ought to be a professor in some college or other. But the North made no provision for George; and moreover, by following the stupid paths which it did, we in the South found it impossible to do the right thing by the Negro. We have never forgotten the golden spitoons and the diamond-studded gavels.

"The entire post-bellum period made no sense. As long as the North did not kill each and every white man who came back from the front, there was no use in preaching the doctrine of equality between white and black. It was a meaningless lot of words. Not even northern baynots and northern laws could emancipate the Negro: it was a hopeless job, surely hopeless in less than a hundred years. But it's a damn shame about George: I could cry when I think of what a bad break he has gotten.

"And as the years pass, the situation gets worse. Factories, newspapers, movies, and agitators have started in getting the black behemoth to move, but as it does, the roar becomes louder and more terrifying. Let me tell you what happened only last week. George can substantiate my every word.

"We started to drive over to Montgomery, my lady friend lives there. George was at the wheel, and Edward—that's the other Negro attendant—sat in front, with him; I was alone in the back. A half hour or so after we had started, a horn blew and for one reason or another, George did not pull over: we were traveling at a fair clip. A few seconds later, the horn blew again, but George continued to hug the middle of the road. It blew for the third time, and we finally, got out of the way. At the car from behind passed, two big Negroes swore at us.

"I told George to overtake them. For the next twenty minutes the chase was on. To this day, I don't understand how both cars held the road. Our old Packard finally overtook them and in passing we forced them into a ditch. I got out and started to walk back to their car. In approaching, I noticed that the one Negro sat with a pistol in his hand while the other one had a rifle by his side. I stepped on the running board and took the pistol away, and then turning it in my hand, swung the butt into the Negro's face. The smash broke his nose and knocked out several of his teeth. Then, I leaned over and grabbed the rifle and after a few parting words about Negroes cursing white men, I walked back to my car and drove off. I later sold the two guns for forty dollars.

"Now, please don't think for a moment that I was brave: I acted as I did because I could not have acted differently. It was pure instinct. After all, if I had let those Negroes get away with it, I could never have felt secure about leaving my mother or sister at home. Once insult a white man, next time a lady. And if you ask why they didn't shoot, for they surely had ample time, well all I can tell you is that these Negroes recognized that I was a real Southerner. Now it is an old tradition in these parts that a white man always kills his Negro assailant before he dies, and if there should happen to be any slip, the white man's relatives and friends will take care of the matter within an hour. George and Edward? We never mentioned the incident.

"Once again, I blame the North. How can you expect 'a nigger' to act differently, especially after he gets liquor into his system, when he has been listening to these Northern communists and agitators tell him that he is just as good as white folk. Do you know that rumor has it that twelve Negroes were mysteriously shot in this very city during the past month, and the police have not found one of the murderers. And they're not going to. Maybe they did the shooting themselves. And it's all because the North is inciting these darkies to do crazy things. No use worrying about the law when the gun and the noose works so much more effectively. After all somebody has to be master, and frankly we intend to remain on top.

"But I don't know how long that'll be. The old times have changed a lot. Now take me: I love poetry and hate Hollywood; I like to hunt and drink and don't care a damn for stock markets and football. Our ideals are disappearing as quickly as our tastes are changing. For instance, we have always believed that our women should remain virgins until they married; that's fundamental to our whole approach. But one need only go over to Mobile, which isn't very far, to see how different things really are. Last winter I kept house there with a woman. We were accepted in the best society, and nobody dreamt of referring, much less objecting, to our relationship. That's the French influence of course, but things are also starting to change around here.

"The other cornerstone of our society is the sacredness of a man's word. Among gentlemen it is never necessary to sign papers; the spoken word suffices. Some vestiges of that tradition still remain. A few months ago, my father visited Atlanta for the first time in twenty years. He went to his old tailor and ordered two suits and a coat to be sent home. The only security which was asked or given was his name.

"But my Mammie is even more typical of the good old days. She has been in our family since the day of her birth, and she is now seventy-six years of age and has been working for us for the last seventy-three years; started as a tot to assist her mother when she waited upon my grandmother. Now Mammie brought me up; I hardly remember my mother who like most ladies in the South remained aloof from the world and life. Mammie might eat like a pig, but she taught me table manners. It was she who instilled in me a respect and love for the ideals of my class. In fact, she had complete charge of me; in fact she had complete charge of the household.

"Now you will probably think that we exploited Mammie in the most shameless fashion, for she never really received a salary. When she wanted a dollar or two she asked for it; when she needed a dress or two she shopped for it. She could not sign her name, but she was able to draw a cross which the storekeepers never failed to honor for they knew right well, that the master of the house would sell the family heirlooms if Mammie's purchases could be paid for in no other way. I should guess that Mammie received two dollars a month in cash and about another two dollars in goods. It sure looks as if we exploited her, but we never realized it and she never realized it. Her life was only a reflection of our lives: She was happy and we were happy.

"But this all belongs to the past. Mammie has no successors and she needs none, for the culture of which she was a part is no more. And though it sounds crazy, yet I feel it in my bones that the day is not very far off when Mammie's relatives, George and his friends will rule this country for they alone are a virile people and will not go to seed.

"Well, it's time to lock up. In the morning you take route 71 until Pleasantville, and then 66. Best way to get out of town, is straight out 14th Street. Goodnight, and next time you come into these parts, I hope that the family treasury will be a little fuller; sure would love to take off a week and show you the *real, old South*."

Non Capisco

The lunch wagon looked like the most inviting place in a very uninviting town. But who cared; I only wanted a bite of breakfast, and an opportunity to glance at the morning paper. The proprietors were Italians and hence had introduced the European custom of supplying their patrons with newspapers. I ordered, and then delved into the first section of the *Kansas City Star.* The first page carried a speech of Mr. Tugwell in which he explained that the Brain Trust was vitally interested in preserving American liberties. Murders, local political news, and the like competed with the assistant secretary of agriculture. I settled in to read his speech to the end.

The orange juice arrived and disappeared without ceremony. The eggs and toast came later. I noticed that the waitress tried to catch my attention, possibly she wished to apologize for keeping me waiting, but I continued to read. The toast and eggs disappeared and the coffee made its appearance. But the girl was also there and this time she could not be ignored. She was determined to attract my attention. I looked up. "Oh, mister—I'm sorry keppa you waiting—but the kids, you knowem dey had de pectures: here they are now—very, very sorry you hada read dat odder stuff in paper, but here is de funnies now."

The Depression

"It's the like of you who ruin a poor woman. Now, don't try to fool me: I know that you brought in a girl last night and you got one in there now! And I rented the room to you alone. Damn nerve of you to bring people in here to sleep with you, and ruin the reputation of my hotel. Now, I'm telling you get out, and get out quickly. What...you offer to pay me twenty-five cents extra, well you sure are a smarty. Well, we'll see. If you're not out of there in five minutes I'm going to call the police, and furthermore I'm going to report you to your superintendent over at the mine. Yes, I am."

Interlude

"So you're trying to give me a check; nix. Who ever told you that I was so dumb. Nothing doing. I want my money. To think of it, you bring in hussies last night and the night before—waking my guests and ruining the reputation of my hotel. Now, you go downstairs right this minute and get that check cashed and if you're not back in ten minutes I'll just turn the matter over to the police. See!

"It's cheapskates like you, brought on this depression."

Lost

Did I ever tell you of the time when I was almost eaten by the bears in Yellowstone? Yes, it was no joke—totally lost and no person within seventy miles.

I was coming east through Montana early in April and decided if possible to go through the park. I didn't know when I would get another chance to see it, and if I could get through I would save several hundred miles of driving. But it was impossible for me to get any definite information as to the condition of the roads. The winter had been very mild and some people assured me that the park was open, that is the roads were cleared of snow; others laughed at me for even thinking that I could get through the park in April. Why, it never opened till the end of June.

Livingstone is the juncture for the north entrance but even here I failed to obtain any reliable information. The chap in the service station thought that the road from Gardner (north entrance) to Old Faithful was open, but he was not certain. I decided to try my luck. At Gardner, I filled my tank to capacity and again inquired about the roads. Would you believe it that the dummy who sold me gasoline didn't know whether I could get through or not. He told me that a half mile down the road, at the official park entrance, there probably would be a sign stating whether through traffic was permissible. Well, sure enough there was a sign: "Road closed for repairs from 9am–3pm." I couldn't afford to hang around and decided to push ahead.

The hot springs at Mammoth—just five miles from Gardner—were interesting, but I was too excited to pay much attention to them. Outside of Mammoth the road continued to climb steeply and the Old Buick had quite a time. Then suddenly the pavement ended and a broken-up dirt road began. Obviously, the repairs were in this neighborhood and I drove the Buick for all it was worth. I assumed that the workmen would not stop me if I acted important. Suddenly, in rounding one of the curves I came face to face with a big truck—a head-on collision was barely avoided. It was an extremely narrow point and there was a drop of some 1500 feet. on the outside. I knew that I was trespassing and therefore hastened to get out of the way. I drove in reverse, hugging the inside of the road. Without warning, the car stopped. I had fallen into a stone pit. Several workmen came to my aid but it was impossible to move the Old Buick. Finally, they tried to maneuver the excavating shovel into position with the aim of lifting the car out. Fortunately, the shovel couldn't get into position. After some forty or more minutes, one of the gang found a piece of cable. The rescue work was delicate for the truck had to avoid running into me, and at the same time had to avoid backing off the mountain. There were no two feet to spare. Well, it worked and I was off. The laborers had been exceedingly good natured about the whole affair and it never struck them to tell me that I was trespassing.

The road improved and soon it became very good. Snow was banked high on either side but for some unknown reason, the road was not wet. For the next hour and a half I failed to see a single living soul; nobody was in the park. And then, just before noon, I arrived at Old Faithful. The geyser was down, but the air was disturbed by hammer blows. A group of carpenters were putting the finishing touches on a new annex to the hotel. The small concession was open, and I discovered that I could eat my lunch there.

It was still a few minutes before noon—and lunch was not served till noon. I walked over to the ranger station to inquire about the geyser and about my route. The ranger told me that the next eruption would take place at about 12:30. He knew more about the geyser than the roads. However, he felt quite certain that I could not continue to the lake for the road crossed the Continental Divide not once but twice; ten feet of snow would not be unusual. He suggested that I double back on my tracks and return to within a few miles of Mammoth Springs—Norris Junction—and there cross over to the east side of the park where the terrain was considerably lower. Now this route would have the further advantage of giving me a chance to see the canyon, which he felt was by far the most beautiful attraction in the park. I could then continue south to the lake and then probably leave the park by the south entrance. He was not absolutely certain that the south entrance was clear but he saw no reason why it should not be. Anyhow I could inquire at the ranger station at the lake (West Thumb).

I gobbled my lunch, watched the geyser, filled my tank and at about 2 p.m. started on my way. The stretch to Norris Junction was completely uneventful just as it had been several hours before, and in fact the road from Norris to the canyon was not exciting though at one point my bumper touched the snow and snapped off as if it had been made of glass.

The ranger was right: the canyon was very beautiful though the total stillness started to get under my skin. There were no carpenters to disturb the quiet. Occasionally, my sightseeing was interrupted by specters of broken axels; I could not forget that I was 40 miles from nowhere.

The trip from the canyon to the lake was not pleasant for somewhere between the two points I noticed that I had used more gas than I had anticipated. Suddenly, I realized that if the South entrance were closed, I would not have enough gas to take me back to Gardner. The safe thing would be to turn around immediately. But the lake was unusually beautiful and I wanted to see more of it. If the South entrance were open I would save an entire day's driving. In the worst eventuality, I would buy a few gallons of gas from the ranger and retrace my steps—it only meant and extra hour and a half. I continued.

I reached West Thumb at about 4:30 and noticed that the road over the Continental Divide to Old Faithful was officially closed. The road south was open. I hastened on for I did not relish the idea of driving in the dark and after all it was seventy miles to the first town. There was no ranger in view, and I did not take the time to search him out. I had enough gas to reach Jackson, at least I hoped I had. The map showed a small settlement between the South entrance and Jackson; doubtless there would be a gas pump there.

Up to this point, the roads had been remarkably good, but now they definitely took a turn for the worse. Outside of West Thumb they became increasingly narrow and wet; moreover, the asphalt covering had almost completely disintegrated. Seventy miles of such driving would be no fun. And then at the end of the third mile, my wheels began to spin. I had no chains, not that they would have been of much use. I knew that the game was up; there was nothing to do but turn around. But turning was no easy matter. The road was very narrow and the Buick was disturbingly large. I got out and looked around. Finally, I found my spot—some 100 yards back. Driving in reverse was comparatively simple, but the right-about-face was difficult. I had overestimated both the size of the cut-out and the hardness of the road. The car started to turn, but it also started to leave the road. Suddenly, the rear wheels began to spin. I continued to leave the road in order to get them to grip. The car was half round. Once again, the wheels failed to take hold. I got out and piled branches under the rear tires. Once again, I got started and this time the car almost completed the circle. But the earth was too soft—the wheels swished in the mud. I backed, and suddenly I slid. The car came to rest in a bog, hopelessly caught and badly tilted.

The trek back to West Thumb was not pleasant. I had to walk rapidly for the hour was getting late. And then, I realized that the rescue would be difficult. No two horses could pull the car out. The ranger would probably have to telephone to Gardner, a towing car would have to come, and I would have to spend the night at West Thumb. The ranger, but I had failed to see him when I drove through. What if there were no ranger? I quickened my pace. There must be a ranger for his colleague at Old Faithful had spoken of him.

Here was West Thumb. I looked for smoke, I looked for life—there was neither. Closer inspection was even more disappointing. The cottages were heavily boarded and locked with big iron bolts. They could have withstood an attack by Indians; and white men were reminded not to play Indians unless they wished to pay $1000 fine and spend a year in jail. There were neither tracks, refuse, nor manure. Obviously nobody had been in these parts for many, many months—probably not since September.

I found a bamboo pole and knocked it against the telephone wires; perhaps, the operator at the other end would become suspicious but who knew whether the line was connected? And even if she heard the noise she would probably think that a group of chipmunks were playing a game.

The sun was racing towards the horizon. I had another half hour of grace—that was all. I tried to think—I wanted to think and then again, I didn't want to think. I was completely conscious of the hopelessness of my situation and yet I was anxious to figure things out more carefully.

I was blocked on the west by the Continental Divide; I was blocked on the south by slush and probably by snow; the east boasted the highest passes in the park and these were assuredly snowbound. The north alone offered the possibility of escape—Gardner, a seventy-mile hike without shelter or food. Well, thank God, I had eaten a good lunch.

Perhaps another foolish tourist like myself would come this way—after all I had gotten through, somebody else might do likewise. Perhaps, a road gang moved in from Jackson every morning—the ranger had mentioned something about repairs. But he was darn unreliable, and furthermore, I didn't see any signs of road work.

I will probably have to walk to Gardner. Well, anyhow, my life isn't in danger. People have often walked seventy miles without food. True, it will get pretty cold at night. I'll just have to break into one of these cottages; and tomorrow night, I will try to break into one of the hotels at the canyon. So, that's that.

The bears! Oh, well they won't do anything to me if I leave them alone. True, the ranger stated that they were in an ugly mood because their hibernation had been cut short, and food was scarce but still they don't attack humans.

No use worrying—and when it's all over, it will make one fine story. Quite a trick to get completely lost in the United States in the year 1934. Funny, how important people really are—even one person could help a lot. Persons—well there weren't any around. Get a drink, you're thirsty.

I slowly came out of my trance and walked down to the water's edge. This was the first time that I noticed how parched I was. The tug-of-war, the walk, and the excitement sure made me thirsty. I stumbled on a crowbar. Well, now I could surely break the ice and get a drink. Moreover, I'll loosen one of the wooden windows of the hut over there—perhaps I'll spend the night in there. The water tasted good, and the hut looked good—the wooden window came off easily.

Only a few minutes to sunset; might as well walk around. Noise! It sounded like the motor of a car—can't be. Must be the wind howling across the lake. After all it's a good size body of water. Noise again! Sure sounds like the sound of a retreating motor—take it easy, plenty of time to go batty on the third day. My God, it is a car.

I started to yell and run as no one has ever yelled and run at the same time. The noise appeared to come from a small hill a half mile or so from the lake. Sure enough, men jumped out from behind trees—honest to goodness men. They looked scared. Later on, I learnt that one of the gang had rushed inside for his gun for he thought that the bears were after me.

But they were not all that surprised to see me for only a few minutes previously they had passed my ditched automobile. They were the road gang of whom the ranger had spoken. One could have spent a week at West Thumb without becoming aware of their existence for their two bunks were completely hidden in the woods.

The boss promised to rescue the Buick after dinner. He asked me whether I had any food, and I told him that I really wasn't very hungry. No—he meant did I have any food in the car, for in that case, he would not have to rescue me. It would take the bears exactly thirty seconds to break in through the road and another thirty seconds to ransack the car in search of edibles. Fortunately, I had no food in the car.

The government fed its men very well. I offered to pay, but the old lady who ran the establishment refused to accept any money. She assured me that it was a pleasure for the government and for herself to feed strangers. A few minutes after dessert, the rescue party started. Four men went along in the big snow truck. It was a bumpy but mighty pleasant ride—at least for me. The actual rescue took not more than three minutes. The cable was attached, the big truck gave several yanks, and out came the Buick. I was told to go back to camp, there was no sense in my waiting around while the truck turned. It took a long while for the truck to make it back to camp. I had begun to fear that it might have fallen into the bog.

I asked the boss to sell me a few gallons of gasoline so that I might be on my way—it was already dark and I would not have refused an invitation to spend the night. But I received neither an invitation nor gasoline. The boss explained that his supply was very low, he just had enough for his own needs. I sympathized with his predicament but assured him that unless he sold me at least four gallons, I would have to overstay my welcome. Finally, the sale was made. Then, I inquired what I owed him for the towing; he stated that a governmental camp could make no charge, but if I desired I might leave something for the men. I had only a large bill which nobody could change and I finally hit upon the idea of writing a check: to this day I am surprised that my bank honored it for my signature looked like nothing I had ever penned before.

It was dark by now, not pitch black but dark. I knew the roads and drove quickly. At the end of the lake, I spotted a large bruin, not ten feet from the road. After that, I drove still more quickly. At the canyon, I missed my turn and almost rolled off the cliff. Searchlight in hand, I found the signposts.

At 10:30, I saw the lights of Gardner. Never were lights more beautiful.